THE OBOE AND THE BASSOON

THE
OBOE
AND THE
BASSOON

Gunther Joppig

Translated from the German by Alfred Clayton

Amadeus Press Portland, Oregon
Reinhard G. Pauly, Ph.D., General Editor

For Maren, Julian Christoph and Fabian Henrik

Published simultaneously with this volume

The Horn
Kurt Janetzky & Bernhard Brüchle

The Flute
Raymond Meylan

The Trumpet
Edward Tarr

This edition copyright © B.T. Batsford Ltd 1988

First published 1988

Translated from the German edition
© 1981 Hallwag AG Bern

Printed in Great Britain

First published in North America in 1988 by
Amadeus Press
9999 S.W. Wilshire
Portland, Oregon 97225, USA

ISBN 0-931340-12-8

Library of Congress Cataloging-in-Publication Data

Joppig, Gunther
    The oboe and the bassoon,

    Translation of: Oboe & Fagott.
    Bibliography: p.
    Includes index.
    1. Oboe—History.   2. Bassoon—History. I. Title.
ML940.J6613   1988   788'.72   88-19278
ISBN 0-931340-12-8

Contents

List of Photographs

Foreword

A few decades ago the oboe and the bassoon were in a manner of speaking the stepchildren of the orchestra, for they rarely appeared in a solo capacity in the world's concert halls. In the last few years there has been a significant change, part of which is due to the fact that contemporary composers have realized the potential of the two instruments (and of the rest of their family) and have written music for them. That the oboe and the bassoon have tended to be overlooked in the concert hall is partly due to the fact that no detailed reference work has been devoted to them. In this book the author describes the two instruments in a succinct and diverting manner, and gives an account of their evolution and ancient origins without neglecting modern developments and trends.

The publishers are to be congratulated on having found an author who not only plays the oboe, the bassoon and the other instruments of the family himself, but who has also made them the subject of his research work, in the course of which he has built up a comprehensive collection of instruments.

Heinz Holliger

Introduction

The oboe and the bassoon belong to the family of double reed instruments. All double reed instruments have a tone generator in the shape of a mouthpiece consisting of two lamellas. The lamellas vibrate when one blows through them, and the gap between the two opens and closes in rapid succession. The resulting periodic vibrations of the air produce a rather shrill, rasping sound that can be higher or lower depending on the width and the thickness of the reeds. Yet this is still a far cry from the top notes of the oboe or the soft and unmistakable hum of the bassoon. Many centuries passed before the oboe and the bassoon evolved from among a whole series of earlier European instruments and reached perfection in their present shapes.

There are two main groups of double reed systems:

1 The double reed is placed directly between the lips, which influences both the quality and the volume of the sound.
2 The double reed is placed in a wind-cap and thus does not come into contact with the player's lips.

The second method seems to be the older of the two. However, it should be added that a wind-cap is not always necessary, for the oral cavity can also assume this function. Numerous instruments were and still are played in this way, though it is impossible to determine precisely those that were the predecessors of the oboe and the bassoon – quite a number of instruments can be played with either a double or a single reed. Thus we shall only glance briefly at possible precursors, our intention being to demonstrate the popularity of reed instruments, and not to attempt to outline a complete evolutionary chain. Historians sometimes tend to portray the course of history as a logical process that begins with the most primitive form and ends with the ideal state. The history of many musical instruments has also been construed in this way. Yet in the process certain parallel developments and instruments which disappeared on account of changes in

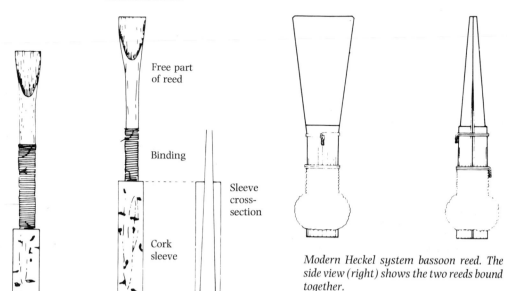

Free part
of reed

Binding

Sleeve
cross-
section

Cork
sleeve

Modern Heckel system bassoon reed. The
side view (right) shows the two reeds bound
together.

German (left) and French oboe reeds (right)
Full size

musical taste are either neglected or deliberately ignored. For
example, the orthodox view of the evolution of the oboe tended to
be that the oboe of the ancient Egyptians was followed by the
aulos of the ancient Greeks, and that this in turn survived in the
shape of the Roman tibia. And the early medieval shawn was for
a long time considered to be the direct precursor of the modern
oboe. Some scholars also applied this evolutionary chain to the
clarinet family.

However, whenever one refers to instruments with a single
reed as clarinet instruments and to those with a double reed as
oboe instruments, one overlooks the fact that in antiquity, in
non-Western cultures and in folk music there were and there still
are numerous instruments that can combine features of both
groups. The indistinct nature of the boundary line between the
two becomes clear when one examines other criteria of the oboe
and clarinet families.

Oboe instruments have a conical bore and sound the octave
when overblown.
Clarinet instruments have a cylindrical bore and sound the
twelfth when overblown.
(According to Riemann, *Musiklexikon*)

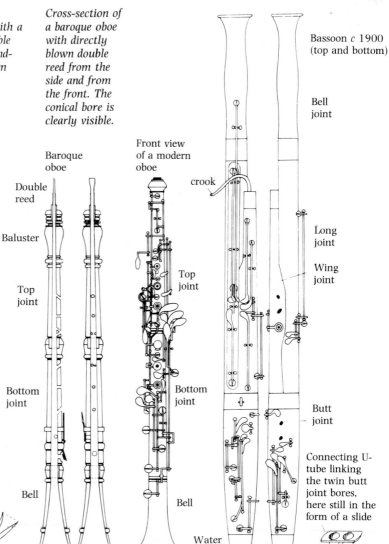

Cross-section of a Renaissance crumhorn with a cylindrical bore. The double reed is protected by a wind-cap and can only be blown indirectly.

Cross-section of a baroque oboe with directly blown double reed from the side and from the front. The conical bore is clearly visible.

Bassoon *c* 1900 (top and bottom)

Bell joint

Baroque oboe

Front view of a modern oboe

crook

Double reed

Baluster

Long joint

Renaissance crumhorn

removable wind-cap

Double reed

Top joint

Top joint

Wing joint

Bottom joint

Bottom joint

Butt joint

Cylindrical bore

Bell

Bell

Connecting U-tube linking the twin butt joint bores, here still in the form of a slide

Water cap

11

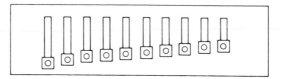

*Reed plate of a mouth organ
with free reeds, front and side
cross-section.*

Yet these straightforward criteria mean that one runs into difficulties when attempting to classify the saxophone and the *tárogató*. Both instruments overblow at the octave in spite of their single reeds, for both have a conical bore. Nevertheless they are considered to belong to the clarinet family.

Attempts continue to this day to replace the troublesome double reed of the oboe and the bassoon with a single reed mouthpiece, yet these instruments do not as a result suddenly become members of the clarinet family. The Berninger oboe (*see p. 85*) and the tenoroon, a higher version of the bassoon, are examples of the use of single reeds on oboe and bassoon instruments. And in the case of Sautermeister's *bass-orgue* the experts disagree to this day on whether we are dealing with a bassoon with a single reed or a bass clarinet in the shape of a bassoon.

On the other hand, quite a few instruments that are held to belong to the oboe group, such as crumhorns, cortholts and sorduns, possess the cylindrical bore characteristic of the clarinet. Raymond Meylan has already described the great variety of ways in which flutes can be blown in his book *The Flute* English edition, Batsford, 1988. In this book we intend to confine ourselves to those instruments which are nowadays assigned to the oboe and bassoon family.

In his postdoctoral thesis *Zur Entwicklungsgeschichte der antiken und mittelalterlichen Rohrblattinstrumente*[1] (Concerning the history of ancient and medieval reed instruments) Heinz Becker has bewailed the lack of exact reproductions of double reeds in antiquity. However, the Museum für Kunst und Gewerbe in Hamburg owns a Greek bowl (Inventarnummer 1962.134) showing a satyr with a double aulos whose wedge-shaped mouthpieces can only be double reeds (*see p. 20*).

Before attempting to elucidate the ancestors of the modern

oboe family, let us recapitulate the various possibilities of producing sounds with the help of beating reeds.

1 Single Reed
(a) percussion reeds (clarinet, saxophone)
(b) free reeds (mouthorgan)
2 Double Reed
Percussion reeds consisting of two halves that beat against each other (oboe, bassoon).

Some readers may consider that the following survey of ancient, medieval and non-Western oboe instruments is too brief; they are referred to the more detailed literature listed at the end of this book.

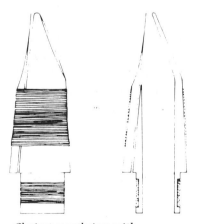

Clarinet mouthpiece with single reed in position.

Table of notes, frequencies and half wavelengths in centimetres

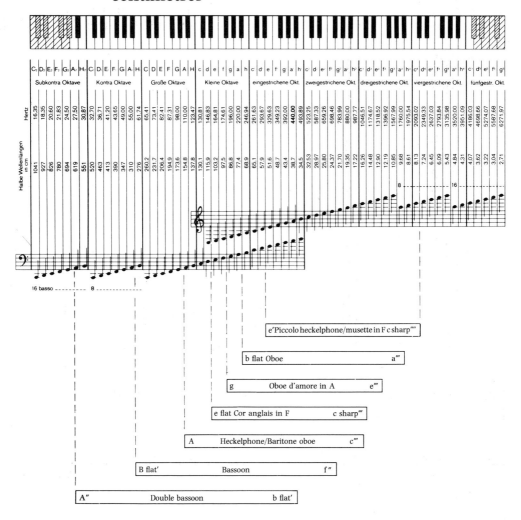

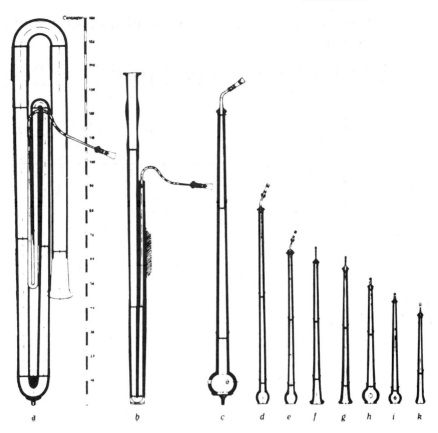

Sizes and bores of modern double reed instruments
Measurements include mouthpiece

All instruments have a conical bore (after Heckel)

Name of Instrument and lowest note		Bore length in cm	Bell shape
a Double bassoon	A''	593	short, flared
b Bassoon	B flat''	259	straight
c Heckelphone	A	138.5	spherical
d Cor anglais in F	e flat	90	pear-shaped
e Oboe d'amore in A	g	72.5	pear-shaped
f Oboe (French)	b flat	66.5	long flared
g Oboe (German)	b	64.5	bell-shaped
h Heckelphone in E flat	d'	52.5	spherical
i Piccolo Heckelphone in F	e'	45	spherical
k Musette in F	f'	42.5	long flared

ONE

Ancient Double Reed Instruments

Oboes in Ancient Egypt

Virtually every book on the history of musical instruments begins by stating that this instrument is the most ancient means of musical expression. Among the natural resources that our ancestors had at their disposal to make bone flutes, percussion instruments or musical bows there were, probably at an early stage, flattened blades of grass which, suitably blown, produced sounds ranging from chirping to buzzing. These, it is thought, were used to imitate natural sounds, to accompany religious ceremonies or simply to satisfy the delight in playing and experimentation that is common to all men.

The first pictorial representations of reed instruments come from around 3000BC, and the oldest double oboe is thought to be an instrument made of silver that was found in the course of excavations at the Royal Cemetery of Ur (*see opposite*). Archaeologists have dated the finds as 2800 BC. Curt Sachs assumed that the complete oboe with three holes was designed for whole-tone scales, and surmised that on account of the narrow bores it was only possible to play notes an octave above the fundamental ones.[2] Overblowing would then have enabled the musician to play the fifth above. This kind of instrument was common all over the Middle East, and is impressively depicted on grave murals from the reigns of Tuthmosis IV (1400–1390 BC) and Amenophis III (1390–52 BC).

A partially preserved mural of a feast in honour of the dead shows the double oboe player from the front – a great exception in Egyptian art – so that we can see quite clearly the two bright reed mouthpieces (*see colour page i*). The hieroglyphics preserve part of the dancing song:

> ... Flowers that Ptah has given and Geb has caused to grow ...
> his beauty is in every body; Ptah has wrought this with his

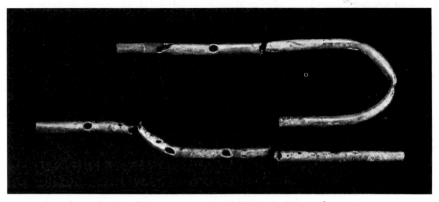

Silver oboes from the Royal Cemetery at Ur (2800 BC). (Pennsylvania, University Museum.)

hands, to delight his heart when the ponds are full of new water and the earth is inundated with its love for him . . .[3]

Another part of the mural shows the double oboe being played together with two long-necked lutes. Other murals depict girls playing double reed instruments together with bow and shoulder harps and long-necked lutes; such pictures indicate that the early oboes were adaptable and changeable. Sachs assumed that the Egyptian harp was enharmonic,[4] its courses being tuned at intervals of a major third with the adjacent semitones, e.g. major third, semitone, major third, semitone, and so on.

This series of notes seems subsequently to have been taken over by the Greeks, who added to the sophistication of the scale by further subdividing the semitone step. The tone holes on Egyptian wind instruments are equidistant and make possible what approximates to whole tone and semitone steps. When playing together with lutes and harps it was no doubt necessary to adjust the tuning by covering adjacent holes. To judge by the pictures that have survived, the reeds were placed directly between the lips, as in the case of the modern oboe, so that it was easier to influence the tone and the pitch than in the case of wind-cap instruments. The musicians probably used instruments of varying lengths, which enabled them to play in different registers. Instruments of this kind are preserved in museums in Cairo, in Leiden, and in the Louvre in Paris.

Female Egyptian musicians. From left to right: clapper, bow harp, double oboe, long-necked lute, lyre and large arched harp.

The Greek Aulos

The Greek poet and musician Pindar (518–436 BC) described the origins of playing the aulos in his Twelfth Pythian Ode, which states that the instrument was invented by the goddess Pallas Athene after Perseus had beheaded Medusa.

> That son of Danaë, by him who, we aver, was begotten of a shower of gold. But, when the maiden goddess had released her liegeman from these labours, she essayed to invent the many-voiced music of auloi, that so, by aid of music, she might imitate the cry exceeding shrill that burst from the ravening jaws of Euryale. 'Twas the goddess that found it: but, when she had found it for the use of mortal man, she called it the 'many-headed tune', that glorious incentive to contests where the folk foregather, – that tune, which oft swelleth forth from the thin plate of brass, and from the reeds which grow beside the fair city of the Graces, in the holy ground of the nymph of Cephisus, to be the true witnesses to the dancers. But, if there be any bliss among mortal men, it doth not reveal itself without toil; yet a god may bring that bliss to an end, verily, even today. That which is fated cannot be fled; but a time shall come which, smiting with a stroke that is unforeseen, shall grant one boon beyond all hope, but shall withhold another.[5]

The ode was written around 490 BC for Midas of Akragas (Agrigentum) after he had won the aulos-playing contest at the Pythian Games in Delphi – the most famous competition next to the Olympic Games (*see illustration*). The ode not only tells us something about the significance of aulos-playing, the invention of which is ascribed to the favourite daughter of Zeus, but also

The court orchestra of Susa (Persia): harps, double oboes or clarinets, percussionists and singers (661 BC).

about the sound and expressive qualities of the instrument. Its music was 'many-voiced' and capable of imitating a 'cry exceeding shrill'. The material of the instrument – 'thin plate of brass' – and the places where the best reed wood grows are also mentioned. (Instruments made of wood, bone and ivory have also been found.) The aulos seems originally not to have been a typically Greek instrument, for Homer (eighth century BC) only refers to it in the *Iliad* when describing the conversations of the Trojans:

> And whensoever he [Agamemnon] looked toward that Trojan plain, he marvelled at the many fires that blazed in front of Ilios, and at the sound of auloi and syrinx, and the noise of men.[6]

And further on we are told:

> And young men were whirling in the dance, and among them auloi and phorminxes [four-stringed lyres].[6a]

A marble statuette of a player with a double instrument, possibly with a double reed, has survived from the time of the Cycladic civilization (3000 BC). Yet if the aulos was still regarded as being foreign at the time of Homer, it later became the most important instrument of the Greeks apart from the kithara (a lyre-like string instrument), and was played on all sorts of occasions. Subsequently the learned began to disapprove of it on account of its connection with the excesses of the Dionysus cult. Hesiod (seventh century BC) mentions the profession of aulos-playing:

Ancient Double Reed Instruments

Left: Detail of an Attic red-figure bowl by the Ambrosios painter (c 510–500 BC) A satyr is holding a double aulos in his left hand. The wedge-shaped double reeds can be seen quite clearly. (Museum für Kunst und Gewerbe, Hamburg.)

Below: Part of a relief from the school of Praxiteles (c 320 BC): the competition between Apollo Kithardos and the aulos-playing Marsyas. (National Museum, Athens.)

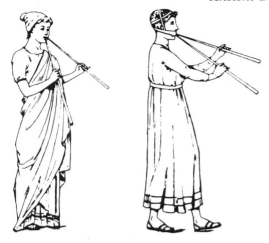

Double aulos players without (left) and with phorbeia (right).

> Then again on the other side was a rout of young men revelling, with auloi playing; some frolicking with dance and song, and others going forward in time with an aulos-player and laughing. (Shield of Heracles)[6b]

Herodotus (fifth century BC) provides us with further interesting information on this point in his *Histories:*

> Moreover the Lacedaemonians are like the Egyptians, in that their heralds and aulos-players and cooks inherit the craft from their fathers, an aulos-player's son being an aulos-player, a cook's son a cook, and a herald's son a herald . . .[6c]

The Lacedaemonians (or Spartans) even used aulos players to maintain the morale of their troops in combat, as transpires from a description by Thucydides of a battle in the *Peloponnesian War:*

> At length the two armies went forward. The Argives and their allies advanced to the charge with great fury and determination. The Lacedaemonians moved slowly and to the music of many aulos-players, who were stationed in their ranks, and played, not as an act of religion, but in order that the army might march evenly and in true measure, and that the line might not break, as often happens in great armies when they go into battle.[6d]

The use of the aulos in such diverse contexts can only really mean that there must have been various different kinds of instrument, the volume, register and tone colours of which were appropriate to the different uses. Though this was probably the case, it is

21

difficult to subscribe to the view that the various kinds of aulos were all played with the same kind of mouthpiece. In the nineteenth century the aulos was often held to be a flute, though research carried out towards the end of the century came to the conclusion that it could only be an oboe instrument with a double reed. In his postdoctoral thesis, Heinz Becker attempted to show that, with very few exceptions, the aulos was equipped with a beating reed of the kind nowadays employed on the clarinet. Yet hardly any of the numerous pictures on vases permit us to come down with certainty in favour of one or the other method. The whole matter is further complicated by the fact that the aulos was often played with a *phorbeia* (or mouth-wrap). This manner of playing points to the fact that the reed was placed in the oral cavity in order to use this as a kind of wind-cap; the phorbeia prevented the cheeks from puffing up too much.

From the writings of Plato (427–347 BC) we learn more about the high level of artistry and virtuosity that instrument makers and musicians had attained. The aulos is described as being the most versatile of instruments, and able to be played in all the modes. A description of this kind of aulos has survived from late antiquity. In the *Guide to Greece* Pausanias (second century BC) says of Thebes:

> There is also a statue of Pronomos, an aulos-player who quite captivated nearly everyone. Until then aulos-players had three kinds of aulos, one sort for the Doric mode, a different sort constructed for the Phrygian mode, and a different sort again for the Lydian mode. Pronomos was the first to think of auloi that could be used for every kind of mode, and the first to play such utterly different tunes on the same auloi.

Attic red-figure bell-shaped crater by the Christie master (440–30 BC). This kind of vessel was used at banquets to mix water and wine. Next to the lyre player there is a courtesan playing a double aulos. (J. Paul Getty Museum, Malibu.71.AE.250.)

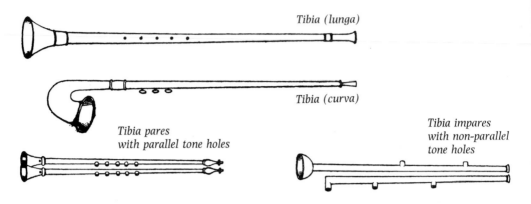

Tibia (lunga)

Tibia (curva)

*Tibia pares
with parallel tone holes*

*Tibia impares
with non-parallel
tone holes*

The Roman Tibia

What has been said of the aulos also applies to the Roman tibia, which was just about as much a Roman invention as the aulos was a Greek one. The Romans probably took this instrument over from the Etruscans, who called their double pipe instrument *subulo*. The players' tasks were numerous; they had to accompany both the preparation of food and the whipping of slaves. In Rome the tibia eventually became the principal instrument and was played on all sorts of occasions. The high social standing of tibia players proves that the musicians were evidently rather popular; the privileges they enjoyed tell the same story. They were members of a special guild; and 'to the privileges extended to (the guild) by the state belonged feasting at public expense in the Temple of Jupiter on the Capitol (the patron goddess was Minerva), and the carnevalesque festival in long gowns and masks on 13 June to commemorate the legendary players' strike on the occasion in 309 BC when an attempt was made to abolish the privilege'.[8]

As early as 451 BC the twelve-table law regulating the relations between the plebeians and the patricians contained provisions stating that only ten *tibicines* were allowed to be present at funeral ceremonies. This law not only proves that tibia music was very widespread, but also that Roman musicians played in groups of more than one instrument. Unfortunately the Roman pictorial depictions of music are not on the same level as the detailed and informative pictures on Greek vases; Roman reliefs and mosaics are inferior to Greek paintings when it comes to the depiction of details.

Although the music of antiquity must be considered lost – only a few fragments have survived, and even these are not precisely notated – we are justified in assuming that there was a high standard of musicianship. The literature on this subject has repeatedly asserted that the tone of the aulos and the tibia was shrill and piercing, yet in all probability this was not always the case. It is true that loud and raucous tibiae were used in the orgiastic music accompanying the worship of Bacchus and Cybele, which favoured the use of a curved version (*curva tibia*). The *tibia phrygiae* consisted of two tubes, one of which had a curved bell; the Dionysus mosaic in Cologne shows this version quite clearly. The *tibia serranae* or *lydiae* had two straight tubes; these two versions were employed in the art music of the theatre, accompanying sung passages and dances.

In the Hellenistic epoch, which began after the final subjugation of Greece around 150 BC, many Greek artists were taken into captivity by the Romans. They had a profound influence on cultural life. The virtuosity of the Greeks and the skill of Roman instrument makers led to the creation of a sophisticated instrument that had the technical refinements required for the various musical styles. The tone holes could be closed and opened by means of metal bands, enabling the musician to play a number of different scales. The Dionysus mosaic seems to show the player on the point of retuning the instrument. These metal bands were known as *bombyker*. In addition to this one can make out knobs, the significance of which has not been convincingly clarified; they may have served to close tone or resonance holes, which could be reopened when required. In Egypt musicians had used wax in a similar way. (To this day oboists and bassoonists use wax to narrow down the tone holes of out-of-tune notes in order to correct the intonation.)

The Roman instrument makers were already masters of the art

of producing and bending metal tubes – a technique that was only rediscovered around 1500.[9] Metal tibiae of this kind, which could be clearly heard at a distance, were used together with water organs to accompany the gladiators in the arena. The makers were also able to produce exact bores, and made tibiae of hardwood and even of ivory. It is easy to understand why the early Christian church did not care for instruments to the sound of which many of its members met their deaths. The Fathers of the Church preferred sacred vocal music to instrumental music, and as a result the tibia virtuosos, who had once been held in such high esteem, sank to the lowest social level. As guardians of a heathen tradition they were often denied the sacraments, lodgings and protection. Yet in spite of the fact that many cultural achievements were irrecoverably lost after the fall of the Roman Empire, the double instrument tradition survived into the Middle Ages.

TWO

The Oboe and the Bassoon in Non-Western Countries and Cultures

Double reed wind instruments are found almost everywhere in the world. In nature tubes in the shape of bones, horns or bamboo only occur up to a certain length (60cm tends to be the limit), and thus only instruments in the soprano register which did not involve the complicated task of joining up smaller tubes could be made. For this reason wind instruments in the tenor or even the bass register are few and far between.[10]

Double reed instruments usually have a round disc at the point on the upper joint where the reed begins. The lips are pressed against the disc so that the reed can vibrate freely in the oral cavity. Pictures show that musicians tend to play with puffed-up cheeks, circular breathing being an essential part of the playing tradition. The length and tone colour of the smaller models correspond roughly to the European musette in F. The tone of these instruments should on the whole be thought of as shrill, even piercing. It hardly needs to be said that they are always an expression of the musical predilections of the particular civilization in question. Whereas double reed instruments are extremely popular in all Asian countries, they are rarely found among the native inhabitants of South and North America, who tend to favour flutes. The *kena* in particular has become well-known in the recent past. Shawms were first introduced into this part of the world by the conquistadores, and later combined with local native instruments. Mexican bandas nowadays include the *chirimia*, an instrument brought over by the Spaniards. In the seventeenth and eighteenth centuries there were Brazilian bands called *charamelleyros* – the name itself indicates that they included shawms.

Oboe instruments are widespread all over the Middle East. An instrument called *zamr-el-kebir* (the name could be translated as 'large oboe') has the same range as our normal oboe. The smaller model is called *zamr-el-soghair* and has the same range as the

27

So-na, a Chinese oboe. (Historisches Museum, Berne.)

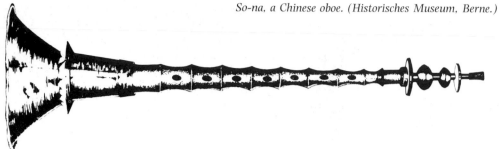

small musette. (*See p. 82, no. 1.*) In Persia the oboe is also called *zamr* or *zourna*.

Oboe-like instruments are also popular throughout India. The name of an instrument called *kalama*, an oboe with a range from f′ to f″, points to the Latin word *calamus* (reed). The *shahnâî* is of interest in that it can be played singly or in pairs, reminding us directly of the Greek aulos and the Roman tibia. Another kind of oboe is called *nyâstaranga*.

Various kinds of oboe still exist in China. The names and models differ from province to province. One instrument is called *kuan*; another version of this is the *kuan-tzu* or *pi-li*, and third form is called *so-na*. Tibet is usually associated with trumpets, but it also possesses an oboe known as *gya ling*. Oboes also occur in Thailand and Korea: a Thai version is called *pî*. In Indochina there are three kinds of oboe. *Cái ken môt* has one tube, whereas *cái ken dôi* has a double tube. These two types have a cylindrical bore, whereas a third kind, *cái ken loa*, has a conical one.

In Japan the Court musicians play the *hichiriki* to this day. It is a high-pitched instrument with a piercing tone, and is used in *gagaku*, the oldest polyphonic music in existence. Nowadays the Court musicians can also play the modern oboe, and listeners at Court concerts are often surprised by the fact that, after playing a piece from the traditional repertoire, the musicians exchange the ancient instruments for modern Western ones and proceed to perform a symphony by Mozart or Beethoven. Yet Western instruments are increasingly endangering the survival of native forms: in Arab countries, according to one ethnologist, it is nowadays difficult to buy an instrument that was actually made to be played. Many instruments are merely make-believe, more or less accurate reproductions produced for the tourist market, and cannot even be played by good native musicians.

In the folk music of these countries the traditional instruments have been rendered obsolete and the accordion has taken the place of wind instruments. Similarly, in India the violin often

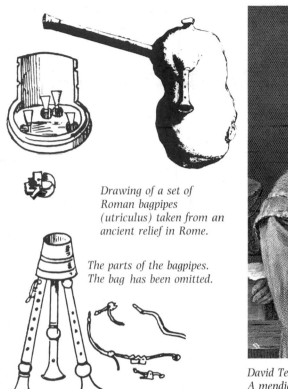

Drawing of a set of
Roman bagpipes
(*utriculus*) taken from an
ancient relief in Rome.

The parts of the bagpipes.
The bag has been omitted.

David Teniers (1610–90).
A mendicant musician with bagpipes. (Gunther
Joppig Collection.)

replaces the *vina* and *sitar*. This is also true of Europe, where it is
rather difficult to find an instrument maker who is still able to
make an instrument in the traditional way. In the recent past
there has been a renewed interest in folk music, particularly on
account of certain soloists such as Gheorge Zamfir (who plays the
panpipes). Musicians like him have become well-known through
recordings, favourite combinations being panpipes and organ,
tárogató and organ, and bombarde and organ. Yet here one is not
dealing exclusively with true folk melodies; much of the material
has been distorted by the influence of Western art music.

We have not as yet mentioned the bagpipe, which in essence is
also an oboe instrument. The experts still disagree about whether
it was known to the Romans – certain references make one
believe that this was so. In the bagpipe the double reed is not
placed directly in the mouth, but in a wind-cap; this in turn is
supplied with air from the bag, which is either refilled like a
bellows with the movement of the arm, or continually resupplied
with air through an additional tube placed in the mouth.

29

THREE

The Diversity of the Middle Ages and the Renaissance

Whether or not the aulos and the tibia were brought to Europe by the Arabs in the Dark Ages must remain an open question in view of the lack of hard evidence, though in his book *The Rise of Music in the Ancient World: East and West*[11] Curt Sachs showed that Greek music theory lived on in Islamic music; and the Nestor of English organologists, Francis W. Galpin, considered the Irish single and double reed instruments without a flared bell to be the direct descendants of the Roman tibia.[12] From the time of the Crusades onwards the instruments used by medieval wandering musicians consisted of wind, string and percussion instruments whose origins lay in Byzantine, Asian and ancient European cultures. These itinerants – they included Arab, Persian, Turkish and even African musicians – took their instruments and repertory all over Europe. Whereas the strange oriental style had little influence on Western music, the instruments proved to be very influential indeed.[13]

By referring to hitherto neglected sources, Heinz Becker was able to show that the Roman tibia continued to be played in French monasteries in the Carolingian epoch,[14] and on this basis came to the conclusion that in secular music its use must have been even more widespread. In his *Etymologiae* the theologian, philosopher and historian, Isidore of Seville (*c* 560–636), described the double tibia and an instrument consisting of a single pipe, which he called *calamus*. This Latin term, as we have seen, means reed or blade of grass. The German *Schalmei*, the Indian *kalama* (which has already been mentioned), the English shawm, the Old French *chalemie* and the Old Spanish *chalemel* can all be traced back to this common root. The shawm is not an instrument *per se*, but rather a whole genre of instruments which are played with either single or double reeds. A characteristic feature is the flared bell. Originally no distinction was made between high and low instruments. The players were usually

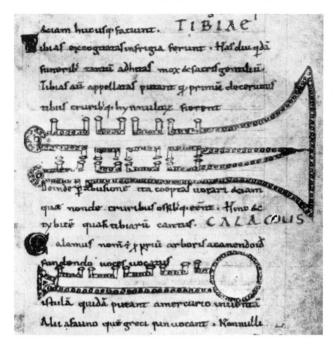

Part of a page of the Etymologiae *of Isidore of Seville (Tibiae, calamus).*

called pipers, though initially they were referred to as jongleurs (i.e. jugglers), which leads us to suspect that wandering minstrels also practised other arts.

According to the *Livre Mestiers* from fifteenth-century Bruges a *gokelare* or jongleur could play

> *ghitteernen, herpen,*
> *salterien, orghelen,*
> *rebeben, trompen, chiphonien,*
> *scalemeyden, bombaren*
> *cornemusen, floyten, douchainen*
> *ende nacairen.*[15]

In other words, the musician was able to play the guitar, the harp, the psaltery, the organ, the rebec, the horn, the hurdy-gurdy, the shawm, the bombarde, the cornemuse, the flute, the dulcian and the timpani; and probably varieties of the same. The guitar, harp and psaltery were plucked instruments, whereas the rebec[16] was a bowed instrument, and the hurdy-gurdy[17] a string instrument in which a rotating wheel took the place of the bow,

31

Woodcut by an unknown master: singers and musicians with trumpet, bagpipe, pommer, harp and lute entertaining a bathing party.

Below: Woodcut by Hans Burgkmair, 1516. A carriage with wind players (trombone, pommers and crumhorns) from 'The Triumph of the Emperor Maximilian I' (1459–1519).

and on which the melody was played on a keyboard. The organ mentioned was most probably the portative,[18] which was widespread in the Middle Ages and the Renaissance. Judging by old pictorial representatives, the musician played the keys with one hand and attended to the bellows with the other. Shawm, bombarde, cornamuse and dulzaina were double reed instruments which we will examine in greater detail below. On the use of flutes and timpani in the epoch the reader is referred to Volume Four of the German Schott series, *The Flute* by Raymond Meylan (English edition, Batsford, 1988) and Volume Eight, *Percussion* by Friedrich Jacob.

The list of instruments suggests that the minstrel was indeed versatile, and this was of great importance, for he had to be able to provide appropriate music for all sorts of occasions.

Long journeys and rambles, battles, festive banquets, indeed even bathing or going to church – aristocrats preferred to do all this to the accompaniment of music. The wandering minstrel who was able to supply this (music) was at the centre of things, a welcome visitor both in the room where children were born, at weddings or at the deathbed. He could accompany the ceremonies of the state, or the toiling peasant or busy artisan.[19]

This quotation from a postdoctoral thesis emphasizes the extent to which the life of medieval man was surrounded and filled with music.[20] After having evaluated hundreds of dispersed sources, the musicologist Walter Salmen noticed links that other scholars had previously overlooked. By concentrating on music preserved by means of notation, they had only pursued research in those areas where people had been able to write – in the monasteries. For this reason the emphasis was one-sidedly placed on vocal music. Yet the large number of pictures of musicians points to the intensive cultivation of instrumental music throughout the

Wilhelm Liefrinck (c 1490–1542). Burgundian pipers from 'The Triumph of the Emperor Maximilian I'. Pommer and trombone players.

Middle Ages, even though few purely instrumental pieces have come down to us.

The learned music theorists despised the musicians, their music and their instruments; and precise descriptions of medieval musical instruments are just as rare as the original instruments. The most comprehensive source of information about the end of the Middle Ages and of the Renaissance is the second volume of Michael Praetorius's (c 1571–1621) *Syntagma musicum*, 'De Organographia'.[21] In this work the composer and theorist made an attempt to classify the various instruments, to describe them, and to explain their musical use. In this respect the volume represents an early instrumentation tutor.

In the second part, ten of the 15 chapters in the section entitled 'Blasende Instrumenta' deal with various kinds of double reed instruments:

Das X.Capittel	Pommern/Bombart/
	Bombardoni:Schalmeyen
Das XI.Capittel	Fagotten:Dolcianen
Das XII.Capittel	Sordunen
Das XIII.Capittel	Doppioni
Das XIV.Capittel	Racketten
Das XV.Capittel	Krumbhoerner
Das XVI.Capitel[*sic*]	Corna-Muse
Das XVII.Capitel	Bassanelli
Das XVIII.Capitel	Schryari
Das XIX.Capitel	Sackpfeiffen[22]

All the instruments mentioned (and the flutes and brass instruments) formed consorts – nowadays we might say families.

According to Praetorius, only the two treble instruments were known as shawms – 'those that have no brass key'. The sizes were as follows:

high treble shawm
treble shawm
Small alto pommer
Large alto pommer
Basset or tenor pommer
Bass pommer
Great bass pommer

The larger pommers had up to four keys, which extended the range downwards. When all is said and done the great bass pommer with its astounding length of 2.75 metres reached down to low F. The Musikinstrumentenmuseum in Berlin owns a consort of sixteenth/seventeenth-century pommers which come from the Marienkirche in Danzig (Gdansk) and the Wenzelskirche in Naumburg.

Right: Recording session with a great bass pommer (Photo: Archiv Produktion.)

Below: Consort of pommers. Sixteenth- and seventeenth-century instruments from the Marienkirche in Danzig (Gdansk) and the Wenzelskirche in Naumburg. From left to right: treble, alto, alto with additional key, tenor, great bass, bass, tenor, alto. (Musikinstrumenten Museum, Berlin.)

According to Praetorius the Italians called the bass pommer *bombardo* and the great bass pommer *bombardone*. Yet the French already referred to the high instruments as *houtbois* and the English as *howeboies*. Galpin showed that the word *howeboie* was being used in place of *shawm* in the reign of Elizabeth I (1533–1603), noting that in 1561 the Queen attended a performance of the tragedy *Gorbuduc, or Porrex and Ferrex*, in which the introduction to the fourth act, which concerns itself with furies and murderers, consisted of a 'musicke of howeboies'.[23]

The habit of using oboes in scenes of ill omen is also to be found in the works of Shakespeare. In *Hamlet* (1600) there is the music accompanying the dumb show in Act 3, scene 2; and in Act 4, scene 3 of *Antony and Cleopatra* (1607) the guards in front of Cleopatra's palace who talk about the naval battle with Caesar's fleet the following day are interrupted by the sound of oboes, which symbolize the fact that Antony will be defeated. Yet in England, according to Galpin, both instruments appear: *hautbois* and *shalms* (1575) and *chalmes* and *howboyis* (1607). He deduced that the higher instrument was called oboe, and the lower one was referred to as shawm. As early as 1665 there is mention of the *tenner hoboy*; Henry Purcell first used it in his opera *Dioclesian* (1690).

In France the word *hautbois* was used sporadically from the end of the fifteenth century onwards to designate high double reed instruments. The name probably means 'high', perhaps also 'loud wood'. In his book on the oboe[24] Philip Bate pointed to two non-musical uses of the word: two villages in Norfolk called Great Hautbois and Little Hautbois; and an English variety of strawberry that bears the name 'Hautbois Strawberry' on account of the way the fruit stands up above the ground. In Spain and France the reports of the arrival of the Philip le Beau in Zaragoza in 1502 mention *trompetas, tambores y haultbois*; in 1532 we hear

of *quatre joueurs de hautbois* in Mons; and in 1579 a certain Claude
de Bouchaudon proudly called himself *haultbois du roy, bourgeois
de Paris.*

Praetorius considered fagott and dulcian to be different names
for the same instrument, yet he states that in England the
Zingelkortholt was considered to be the true dulcian. In his thesis,
the bassoonist and musicologist Albert Reimann[25] made a
detailed study of the various names for the bassoon (fagott –
dulcian – curtall – bassoon – storto). He traced the word *fagot*
back to thirteenth century Old French, where it meant bundle, or
bundle of sticks. In Italy *fagotto* only acquired this meaning
around 1500. Its Latinized form, 'phagotus', was the expression
used by Canon Afranio degli Albonesi for an invention that for a
long time was considered to be a precursor of the bassoon, but
which in reality was a bagpipe with metal tongues. However, it is
unclear why the word bundle should have been applied to a
musical instrument in which two tubes were bored into one piece
of wood, as is the case with the dulcian, for the multipartite
manner of making the instrument first arose towards the end of
the seventeenth century. Praetorius at any rate was not familiar
with this term.

One of the earliest pieces of evidence for bassoons in Germany is
the inventory of the musical instruments belonging to the Fugger
family that Raimund Fugger the younger (1528–69) compiled in
1566. The catalogue lists no less than 13 *fagotti* in addition to
nine shawms, eight crumhorns and two *doltzana*.[26] From old
inventories and from the descriptions supplied by Praetorius, we
see that people always referred to '*der* Fagott', the masculine
form, and not to '*das* Fagott'. In French and Italian *fagoto* and
fagot are also masculine. The neuter form began to gain currency
in the nineteenth century, and today only the traditional
bassoon-making firm of Heckel in Wiesbaden-Biebrich retains
the masculine form.

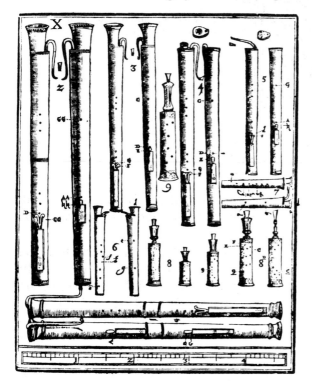

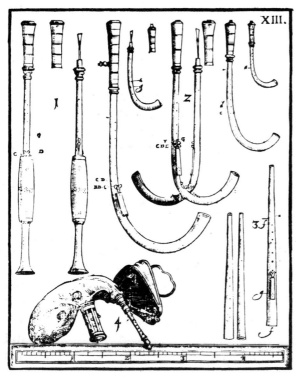

Michael Praetorius: Plates X and XIII with various double reed instruments and cornetts from De Organographia *(1619). Moeck (Celle) assembled the exhibits on page 43 (modern reproductions from the studio department of historical instruments) to correspond to these two plates.*

Cross section drawings of the doppioni at the Società Filarmonica, Verona.

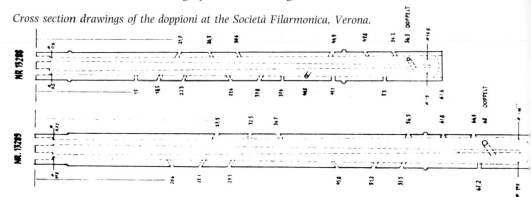

Praetorius lists the following versions of the bassoon: *discant*, *fagott piccolo*, *fagott*, also known as *chorist fagott*, *quartfagott* or double bassoon, and *quintfagott* or double bassoon. Nowadays the last two sizes would be considered small double bassoons: the *quartfagott* descended to G′ and the *quintfagott* to F′. At the end of the chapter devoted to bassoons and dulcians there is an interesting paragraph about a double bassoon then being developed:

> The master/ who made the octave trombones/ is now working/on a large bassoon contra/ which reaches a fourth below the double bassoon, that is to say, an octave lower than the choristfagott/ which is to be able to play a 16 foot C/ if he succeeds/ it will turn out to be a splendid instrument/the like of which has not been seen/ and people will surely marvel at it . . .[27]

As opposed to pommers and dulcians, sorduns have a cylindrical bore, which in acoustic terms makes a stopped pipe of the open conical one. (A stopped pipe sounds an octave lower than an open pipe of the same length.) The sorduns now at the Kunsthistorisches Museum in Vienna, which come from Schloss Ambras, have a surprisingly sophisticated key mechanism. Here the consort also consists of great bass, quint or quart bass, bass and tenor.

Praetorius did mention the *doppioni*, though he never actually saw one himself. It seems that the only instruments to have survived are the two at the *Società Filarmonica* in Verona. The instrument maker Rainer Weber and the former curator of the Germanisches Museum in Nuremberg, John Henry van der Meer, examined and described them in an essay published in *The Galpin Society Journal*.[28] As early as 1953 Anthony Baines had sug-

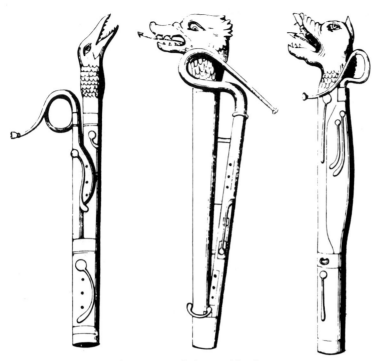

Bass horns or Russian bassoons with dragons' heads.

gested in the same journal that these instruments were probably *doppioni*. Reimann, on the other hand, is of the opinion that the two instruments are an important and hitherto missing link between the *phagotus* and the bassoon, interpreting them as very early examples of the latter. The two adjacent bores widen towards the bottom. It seems likely that the player could change from one side to the other, using a double reed and a crook. The instruments may also have had a wind-cap. On account of the largely equidistant tone holes one body united within it two different instruments of the same kind, i.e. treble/alto, alto/tenor, tenor/bass, bass/great bass. The Verona instruments are of the alto/tenor and tenor/bass type.[29] Attempts to play the restored instruments have shown that two scales really were available.

That such subtle constructions were not unusual is amply demonstrated by the racket family. In the case of these instruments nine parallel holes were bored vertically in a wooden or ivory cylinder and then linked up. The snake-like inner sound holes thus created were then bored into from the outside. The tone holes were in part supplied with raised edges that could be closed with the phalanges. Keys were not required; and the compact construction meant that one could play quite low notes despite the shortness of the instrument. Later rackets had conical bores and a bell. A consort consisted of two great basses, a quint bass, a bass and a tenor. On account of their stout and rather squat appearance they were sometimes called *Wurstfagott* (sausage bassoon). A further variant is the dragon-shaped *tartöld*, examples of which are preserved in the Vienna collection. The practice of adding a dragon's head to a musical instrument continued well into the nineteenth century, particularly in the case of brass instruments.

Crumhorns are just as difficult to make. This family of instruments is also played with a double reed placed in a wind-cap. The narrow cylindrical bore is drilled into the wood while it is still straight. Then it is steamed for some time and bent on a mould. (Instruments consisting of several joints were occasionally made.) The length of time under steam depends on the kind and the thickness of the wood and must be neither too long nor too short. An instrument maker who wishes to make crumhorns must be a very proficient craftsman indeed. Praetorius had seen the following sizes: small treble, treble, alto, tenor, bass, great bass. Although original scoring indications are rare in the music of the sixteenth century, certain pieces were specially written for crumhorns. Thomas Stoltzer (c 1480–1526) noted on a seven-part psalm *Noli aemulari*:

> Had crumhorns in mind and wrote the psalm so that it fits them; not every piece can be comfortably played on them . . .[30]

We do not in fact know what a cornamuse looked like. Modern reconstructions of the instrument resemble straight crumhorns, with the bottom end of the instrument being closed. Its sound is even quieter than that of the crumhorn. Praetorius mentions a consort consisting of bass, tenor, alto and cantus (treble).

Little is known about the *bassanelli* Praetorius depicts and

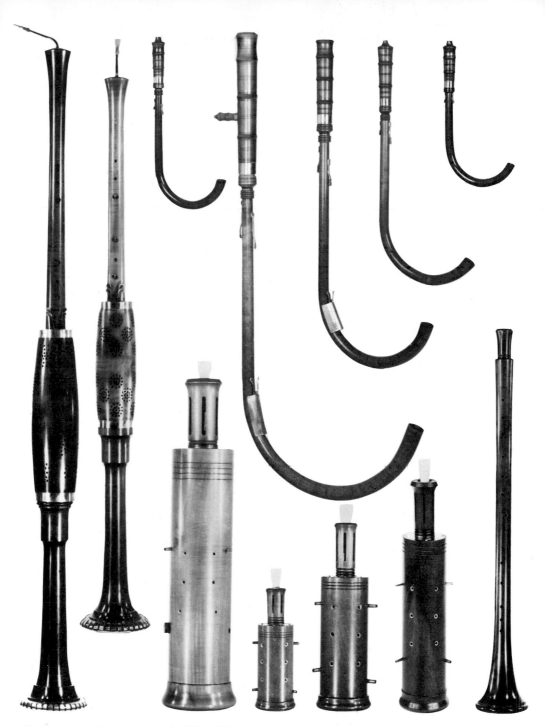

Modern copies of Renaissance double reed instruments:
Pommers: 1. Tenor 2. Nicolo
Crumhorns: 3. Alto 4. Contrabass 5. Bass 6. Tenor 7. Treble
Rackets: 8. Great bass 9. Tenor 10. Basset 11. Bass
Shawn: 12
(Manufacturer: Moeck Verlag + Musikinstrumentenwerk, Celle)

43

*Dulcian and crumhorns at a
recording session. Photo: Archiv
Produktion, Hamburg.*

Heinrich Aldegrever, 1551. Crumhorn players. (Graphische Sammlung Albertina, Vienna.)

describes. He attributed the invention to 'Iohann Bassano, an excellent instrumentalist and composer in Venice'.[31] The instruments depicted – great bass, bass and tenor – have decidedly baroque turnings. The bore was evidently narrower than in the case of the pommers, and with good reeds it was possible by means of overblowing to produce fairly high notes. The sound seems to have been less piercing than that of the *schryari* or *schreierpfeifen*. These were also built as stopped pipes, perhaps even in inverted conical form, and had a wind-cap. They are said

45

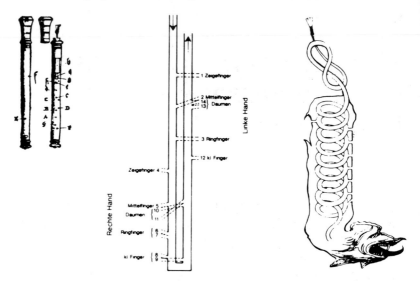

Left: Kortholt from Plate XII. Michael Praetorius, De Organographia (1619).

Right: Schematic drawing of the bore and the tone holes (Moeck).

Far right: Schematic drawing of the tartöld (after Buchner). The name tartöld is a bowdlerization of the Italian torto and the German kortholt.

to have been even louder than the pommers. (Both the tonal characteristics and the name could point to oriental origins.) Praetorius depicts bass, tenor/alto and cantus (treble) instruments.

Whereas no *schreierpfeifen* have in fact survived, there are a few *rauschpfeifen* in the Prague and Berlin collections. They resemble shawms, but have a wind-cap instead of a pirouette to support the lips. Praetorius had little to say about the *kortholt* (short wood). As Georg Kinsky pointed out, the word was applied to many instruments. One of these had a double reed in a wind-cap, and two adjacent cylindrical bores, in this respect resembling the sordun (though the latter's reeds were directly blown).

Common to all the instruments mentioned was the restricted range of a maximum of one and a half octaves. This was compounded by their tonal inflexibility, and meant that many medieval and Renaissance instruments were in the long run unable to satisfy the demands that began to be made on them.

FOUR

The Triumph of the Oboe and the Bassoon in the Baroque Era

In our survey of the history of music we have noticed that the Middle Ages and the Renaissance had at their disposal an unbelievable variety of instruments. Yet the surprising fact remains that this variety did not increase, that is to say, the instruments were not perfected technically. Instead, a process of elimination began which led to many of the double reed instruments already mentioned becoming obsolete. It is interesting to note that the instruments whose blowing technique offered little in the way of changing the tone quality were particularly affected; nor did instruments with a wind-cap survive for very long in the modern age. The gradual relegation to a lower cultural level or even total disappearance of an instrument cannot however be explained simply in terms of its use or the way in which it was played – rather, it should be viewed in the context of the changing ideas which made possible the transition from the darkness of the Middle Ages to the more enlightened spirit of subsequent centuries.

For many hundreds of years instrumental music was overshadowed by vocal music, which was cultivated by the church and thus tended to predominate. Instruments were assigned a subsidiary role, and only a few of them were important enough to require specially qualified musicians. Trumpeters and drummers who served at the courts and on the battlefield were held in high esteem, for they were an expression of temporal might. Yet other musicians were on the whole held in low esteem and often regarded as belonging to the same social class as other itinerants. In medieval manuscripts one often finds musicians depicted next to jugglers. They did not concentrate on one particular instrument, but were generally able to play several. For this reason the kind of specialization which alone makes it possible to achieve the highest standards was impossible.

Those who had the good fortune to be appointed to the post of town musician were better off, for they were able to employ journeymen and apprentices. Municipal musicians had to provide music for all sorts of occasions, and could play almost everything: string instruments for 'soft musick' on festive occasions; and sonorous wind instruments for 'loud musick' in the open. Even today there are a few town pipers who train apprentices to play a variety of instruments and who provide music for all sorts of occasions.

The instrument maker, inasmuch as he specialized in the construction of musical instruments at all, was not held in high esteem. Wind instruments were often made on the side by the local turner, and hardly anybody considered the flute or the shawm to be a work of art. The instruments were simple and made of material found in the local forest. An ornamental turning or some other kind of decoration was rare, and thus instruments did not become too expensive for the run-of-the-mill musician. Instrumental music was still in its infancy, the repertoire consisting mainly of vocal music, which was frequently performed with alternating choral and instrumental passages. The artist as we know him today, a person, that is, who creates individual and unique works of art, did not as yet exist.

This began to change in the transition from the Renaissance to the Baroque. People became conscious of their individuality and began to identify with what they had created. Pictures began to be signed, composers wrote their names at the top of their pieces, and makers inscribed their marks on their instrument. The rise of the artist led to a battle for the favour of the public, and the era of specialization began. The side product of a solid local craftsman or carpenter no longer sufficed. Instruments were now made a long way away, and the first centres of instrument making came into being. Nuremberg was one of the most prominent centres, with makers such as the Denner family, the Oberlenders and the

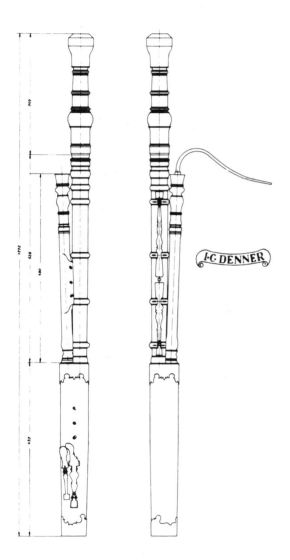

A masterpiece: a bassoon by Johann Christoph Denner (1655–1707), Nuremburg. (Heckel Museum, Wiesbaden-Biebrich.)

HAUTBOIST.

Engraving by Johann Christoph Weigel (1661–1725).

Löhners.[32] Certain centres cannot be identified; we know the makers' names or marks, but we do not know where they worked. Among them were Klenig and Liebav, who figured prominently in the history of the oboe and the clarinet.

Paris was also an important centre. A list from the year 1692 mentions thirteen *maîtres pour le jeu et pour la fabrique des instruments à vent, flûtes, flageolets, hautbois, bassons, musettes, etc.*[33] Among them were members of the Hotteterre and Philidor families, as well as Dupuis, one of whose early oboes is in the Berlin collection.

There were also good makers in Amsterdam and London. In Amsterdam the instruments made by Richard Haka (*c* 1645–1705) provide a good idea of the differences between shawms and oboes. His colleague Jan Juriaensz van Heerde (?–1691) had a shop called 'Gekroonde Fagot' (At the sign of the bassoon crowned) where, according to an old advertisement, he made *fluyten, hoboes, bassons, veltschalmeyen en fluytkonststokken*[34] (flutes, oboes, bassoons, military shawms and artful flutes). Both the oboe and the shawm were still in use, though it is noticeable that the shawm was clearly intended for outdoor use. This function is apparent in the engravings of Johann Christoph Weigel (1661–1725). The poem accompanying the *Hautboist* states:

Away thou rural shawn! My sound shall drive thee hence
I serve right well in time of peace and time of war,
I serve the church and serve at court, where thou art not,
Wine is my reward, and thou must do with yeasty beer,
Thou in the village, I in castles live and towns,
Thou hast but a penny ribbon; I have golden chains.[35]

The period between 1600 and 1750 is usually called the age of the thoroughbass, for the *basso continuo* formed the harmonic and tonal background on the basis of which the concertizing instruments elaborated their lines. A new genre, the opera, also influenced instrumental music, not only because solo monody marked a departure from polyphonic choral music, but also because it specified the accompanying instruments. Thus, in the preface to the opera *Orfeo*, which was performed in 1607, Claudio Monteverdi (1567–1643) clearly stipulated the instruments that made up the orchestra.

The early appearance of the *hautbois* has already been pointed out. Yet it is difficult to say precisely when the oboe was invented, for it is not clear which form of the instrument we are talking about. Nowadays the following criteria serve as the distinguishing features.

	Shawm	Oboe
Body	one-part	3 parts (top, bottom and bell)
Embouchure	Double reed with pirouette	Double reed is placed directly between the lips
Tone holes	Simple tone holes	Third and fourth tone holes doubled
Key protection	Fontanelle, if key present	No key protection
Bore	Wide conical	Narrow conical
Keys	Occasionally one key	3 keys

However, there are tripartite shawms and also oboes which retain the fontanelle of the pommer family (e.g. as does the oboe by Dupuis on page 53, no. 1).

The transformation of the shawm into the oboe was more a process of selection from among various kinds of shawm than an invention as such. It is often said that the inventors were Jean de Hotteterre (died 1691) and members of the Philidor family, who played in the *Musique de la Grande Ecurie* from 1650 onwards. The provision of music at the French court was an old tradition; Louis XI (1423–83), for example, was entertained by 'hautbois, cornemuse et musette'.[36] In the reign of Louis XIV, the Sun King (1638–1715), the making of oboes reached a new peak, and this soon influenced the neighbouring states. The German courts quickly developed an interest in the instrument, and French musicians were appointed to the Court orchestras and to teach

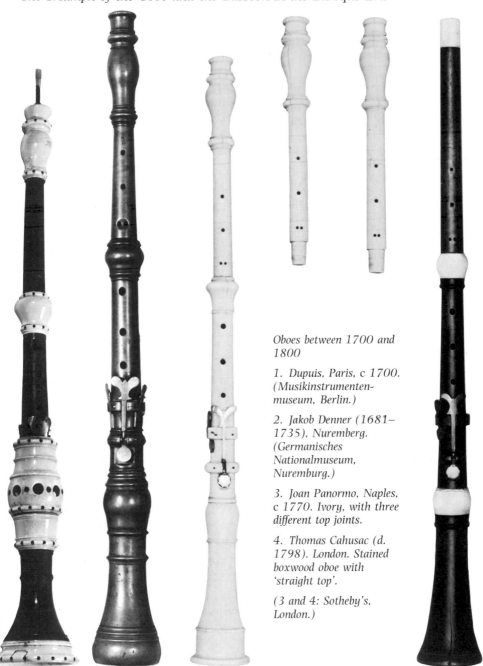

Oboes between 1700 and 1800

1. Dupuis, Paris, c 1700. (Musikinstrumenten-museum, Berlin.)

2. Jakob Denner (1681–1735), Nuremberg. (Germanisches Nationalmuseum, Nuremburg.)

3. Joan Panormo, Naples, c 1770. Ivory, with three different top joints.

4. Thomas Cahusac (d. 1798). London. Stained boxwood oboe with 'straight top'.

(3 and 4: Sotheby's, London.)

March of the Duke of Weissenfels regiment.

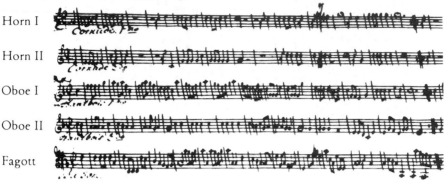

Beginning of a Saxon regimental march from the year 1729. (Staatsarchiv, Dresden.)

their German colleagues.[37] In some regiments the new instrument had been introduced by 1681, e.g. in the principality of Anhalt-Dessau, where there were four German shawm players and a French oboist.[38]

In the reign of Louis XIV, Jean-Baptiste Lully (1632–87) was *compositeur de la musique instrumentale du Roi*. His ballet *L'amour malade* (1657) already made use of oboes, some years before Robert Cambert's (1628–77) opera *Pomone* (1671), which also included oboes. The date of this performance is often said to mark the introduction of the oboe into the orchestra, though Cambert had used the instrument as early as 1659 in his opera *Ariane, ou le Mariage de Bacchus*.

As we have seen, the oboe was quickly taken up in Germany. The term *hautbois* already appears in W.C. Printz's *Musicus Curiosus*, which was printed in Freiburg in 1691; and by the end of the seventeenth century oboes had become an integral part of the orchestra of the Hamburg opera.[39]

The Hotteterres are usually credited with having transformed the one-piece dulcian into a three-piece and subsequently a four-piece bassoon in the second half of the seventeenth century. None of their bassoons seem to be in existence, though four dulcians, four bassoons and a fagottino by the famous German maker Johann Christoph Denner (1655–1707) have survived.[40] The fact that Denner made one-piece dulcians and four-piece bassoons allows us to deduce that the bassoon had already attained its present shape towards the end of the seventeenth century. Although there are far more performance indications for the bassoon than for the oboe, the dulcian was probably widespread right up to the end of the seventeenth century.

Engraving by J. Punt of a picture by P. v. Cuyck jnr (1752). A group of wind players consisting of three oboists, two horn players and two bassoonists. The musicians are accompanying a funeral procession and have decorated their instruments with mourning crape. (Buser Collection, Binningen.)

The French oboe was brought to England by Robert Cambert after he had been deprived of his Académie d'Opéra privilege in 1672 as a result of Lully's intrigues. In 1673 Cambert went to London, where he founded a Royal Academy of Music under the patronage of the music-loving, francophile King Charles II (1630–85). In 1674 he was finally able to mount a performance of his opera *Ariane*, which he had composed 15 years earlier. In the same year Cambert collaborated with Nicholas Staggins (?–1700), an oboist and Master of the King's Musick, in a performance of the latter's masque *Calisto*. It is worth mentioning that for this performance Staggins was able to enlist the services of four French oboists – Paisible, de Bresmes, Guiton and Boutet. Cambert, incidentally, was murdered in 1677, a crime which has never been solved. Of the four musicians mentioned Jacques Paisible (anglicized as James Peasable) (*c* 1650–?1721) built up a considerable reputation as an oboe and recorder virtuoso. After playing in *Calisto* he remained in England, and thanks to his inimitable style of playing the oboe and recorder soon became very popular. Obbligato parts in works by Henry Purcell (1659–95) for the two instruments seem to have been written at his instigation.

55

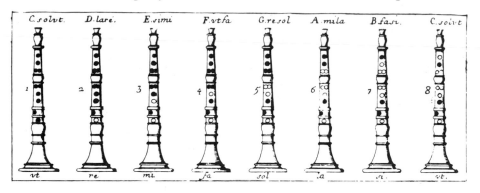

Excerpt from Pierre Freillon-Poncein's fingering chart (1700).

The high regard in which the oboe was held towards the end of the seventeenth century is highlighted by the fact that the first oboe tutors appeared in England before 1700. In France the first important tutor was written by Jean-Pierre Freillon-Poncein. It was entitled *La Véritable Manière d'apprendre à Jouer en Perfection du Hautbois, de la Flûte et du Flageolet.*[41] The range of the oboe is stated to be from c' to d'''. It is noteworthy that the enharmonic changes for each semitone step are included, with different fingerings for the notes c''/d flat'' and b sharp'/c''. This may be taken as proof of the fact that the early oboists were at pains to play in tune.

Music owed much to the French players of the first generation. George Frideric Handel (1685–1759) came across them in Halle, where Michael Hyntzsch's *Hautboisten Companie* had a great reputation. We may assume that Handel composed his six trio sonatas for two oboes for this *companie*. Johann Ernst Galliard (*c* 1680–1749) is also said to have inspired Handel to write works for solo oboe.[42] Galliard was born in Celle and learned to play the instrument with Pierre Maréchal, one of the French oboists who played at the local court from 1681 onwards. At the beginning of the eighteenth century he went to London and probably worked with Handel on a number of occasions. In addition to chamber music for oboe and bassoon Galliard, whose compositions were of course influenced by Handel, wrote a concerto grosso for 24 bassoons and four double basses around 1745.

In the eighteenth century the instrument and those who played it had a more illustrious position in musical life than in the nineteenth and twentieth centuries. The travelling virtuosos were also composers, and they dazzled their audiences with pieces specially written for themselves.

The Besozzi Family

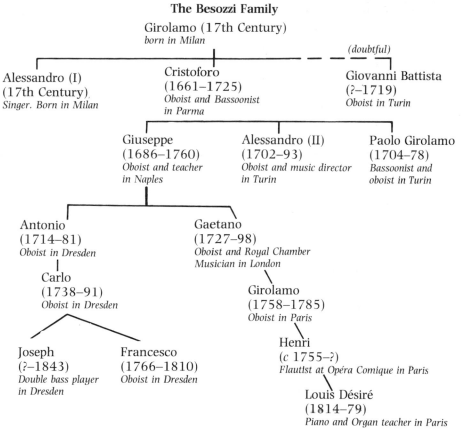

Girolamo (17th Century)
born in Milan

Alessandro (I)
(17th Century)
Singer. Born in Milan

Cristoforo
(1661–1725)
Oboist and Bassoonist
in Parma

(doubtful)

Giovanni Battista
(?–1719)
Oboist in Turin

Giuseppe
(1686–1760)
Oboist and teacher
in Naples

Alessandro (II)
(1702–93)
Oboist and music director
in Turin

Paolo Girolamo
(1704–78)
Bassoonist and
oboist in Turin

Antonio
(1714–81)
Oboist in Dresden

Gaetano
(1727–98)
Oboist and Royal Chamber
Musician in London

Carlo
(1738–91)
Oboist in Dresden

Girolamo
(1758–1785)
Oboist in Paris

Joseph
(?–1843)
Double bass player
in Dresden

Francesco
(1766–1810)
Oboist in Dresden

Henri
(c 1755–?)
Flautist at Opéra Comique in Paris

Louis Désiré
(1814–79)
Piano and Organ teacher in Paris

Giuseppe Sammartini (c 1693–1751) was an oboe virtuoso with an international reputation. The brothers Giuseppe and Giovanni Battista were taught to play the oboe by their father, a French player who belonged to the first generation of oboists. Whereas Giovanni remained a theatre musician in Milan all his life, Giuseppe gave guest appearances in Paris and London. Johann Joachim Quantz (1697–1773), who was himself familiar with the oboe, considered him to be one of the best Italian musicians of his time, and the English music historian Sir John Hawkins (1719–89) 'the greatest (oboist) the world had ever known'.[43]

The Besozzi family formed a whole dynasty of oboists and bassoonists (*see accompanying table*). Cristoforo Besozzi (1661–1725) was oboist and bassoonist in Parma, where he played in the ducal chapel with his sons Giuseppe (1686–1760), Alessandro (II) (1702–93) and Paolo Girolamo (1704–78). Alessandro (II) went on numerous extended concert tours with his brother Paolo. Whereas Alessandro played the oboe, Paolo

Charles Burney (1726–1814). Engraving by Francesco Bartolozzi.

usually played the bassoon, though he could also play the oboe. The many trio sonatas are nowadays mostly ascribed to Alessandro, though some at least will have been composed jointly with Paolo.

The English music historian Charles Burney (1726–1814) has left an account of a visit to the inseparable brothers in Turin in 1770.

> The eldest plays the hautbois, and the youngest the bassoon, which instrument continues the scale of the hautbois, and is its true base. The compositions of these excellent musicians generally consist of select and detached passages, yet so elaborately finished, that, like select thoughts or maxims in literature, each is not a fragment, but a whole; these pieces are in a peculiar manner adapted to display the powers of the performers; but it is difficult to describe their style of playing. Their compositions when printed, give but an imperfect idea of it. So much expression! such delicacy! such a perfect acquiescence and agreement together, that many passages seem heart-felt sighs, breathed through the same reed. No brilliancy of execution is aimed at, all are notes of meaning. The imitations are exact; the melody is pretty equally distributed between the two instruments; each forte, piano, crescendo, diminuendo, and appoggiatura, is observed with a minute exactness, which could be attained only by such a long residence and study together.[44]

Whereas Alessandro (II) and Paolo Girolamo never married, Giuseppe had two sons who both became oboists. Antonio (1714–81) was in Dresden from 1738 onwards, being appointed first oboist in the Royal Chapel on 1 July 1739. Antonio's son Carlo (1738–91) became chamber virtuoso at his father's side at the early age of 17. Antonio's brother Gaetano (1727–98) went

Leopold Mozart (1719–87). Engraving by Jean Baptist Delafosse, 1764.

to Paris via Naples, becoming soloist of the Concert Spirituel. In 1793 he moved to London, the most highly-paid virtuoso of his age, and became principal oboist in the concerts of Johann Peter Salomon (1745–1815), for whom Joseph Haydn (1732–1809) wrote his 12 famous London symphonies. Burney records that he heard him in 1793 as an old, grey man of 65 who still played with extraordinary passion, great expression and utmost precision, and that his tone was the most exquisite he had ever heard.[45]

Mozart and his father visited Turin from 14 to 31 January 1771, shortly after Burney, and probably heard Alessandro and Paolo Girolamo. And Karl Ditters von Dittersdorf (1739–99) considered Alessandro to be one of the best virtuosos of his age.

> The result was, that we had Gabrieli, Guarducci, Mansoli, as singers; Pugnani, and Van Maldre, on the violin; Besozzi on the oboe; Le Clair on the flute; Stamitz and Leutgeb as soloists on the horn; and other eminent players.[46]

Carlo Besozzi (1738–91) became the most famous member of the family. Burney praised both his accomplished playing and the fact 'that he was not only possessed of an excellent understanding, but that he had thought more profoundly concerning the theory of his art, than most practical musicians with whom I have conversed'.[47] Burney heard Besozzi in Dresden in 1772, giving a description of his playing, and Leopold Mozart (1719–87) left an interesting account of him in a letter to his son dated 28 May 1778. The two reports tell us more about what eighteenth-century oboists were able to do than any amount of conjecture. Of particular interest are Leopold Mozart's remarks about his accurate intonation.

> After this, Signor Besozzi played an extremely difficult concerto on the hautbois, in a very pleasing and masterly manner;

yet I must own that the less one thinks of Fischer, the more one likes this performer. However, I tried to discriminate, and to discover in what each differed from the other: and first, Fischer seems to me the most natural, pleasing, and original writer of the two, for the instrument, and is the most certain of his reed; which, whether from being in less constant practice, or from the greater difficulty of the passages, I know not, more frequently fails Besozzi in rapid divisions, than Fischer: however, Besozzi's *messa di voce*, or swell, is prodigious; indeed, he continues to augment the force of a tone so much, and so long, that it is hardly possible not to fear for his lungs. His taste and ear are exceeding delicate and refined; and he seems to possess a happy and peculiar faculty of tempering a continued tone to different bases, according to their several relations: upon the whole, his performance is so capital, that a hearer must be extremely fastidious not to receive from it a great degree of pleasure.

Charles Burney in Dresden, 1772.[47a]

The famous Carlo Besozzi has been here and has played twice at court, each time two concerts of his own composition. His writing, although it smacks a little of the older style, is neatly and soundly worked out and has something in common with that of our Haydn. But indeed his oboe-playing is all that is to be desired and I found it absolutely different from what it was when I heard him play in Vienna. In short, he has everything! Words fail me to describe his precision and the extremely pure tone he preserves in the most rapid runs and jumps. What is particularly remarkable is his ability to sustain his notes and his power to increase and decrease their volume, without introducing even the slightest quiver into his very pure tone. But this *messa di voce* was too frequent for my taste and has the

Beginning of the 12 Variations on a Minuet by Johann Christian Fischer K 189a
(1774).

Wolfgang Amadeus Mozart (1756–1791)

same melancholy effect on me as the tones of the harmonica,
for it produces almost the same kind of sound. Besozzi sends
you his greetings. He is still in the service of Saxony and is only
going to Turin because the King has conferred on him the
rights of citizenship. Otherwise, as he was born in Naples, he
could not claim the right to inherit from his two uncles, one of
whom, the bassoon-player, has just died. I have given him
your sincere greetings and have asked him to convey our
compliments to Abbate Gasparini. Our Archbishop has given
him twenty ducats.

Leopold Mozart to his wife and son in Paris from Salzburg on
28 May 1778.

The Letters of Mozart and His Family. Vol. II. Translated and
edited by Emily Anderson, London, 1938, pp. 798–9.

Johann Christian Fischer, who was also mentioned by Burney,
was born in Freiburg im Breisgau in 1733. In 1757 he appeared
as solo oboist in a concerto by Alessandro Besozzi in Warsaw. As
he was in the service of the Dresden court from 1760 to 1764 we
may assume that his relations with the Besozzi family were close.
In 1765 he went to Italy to study the great singers and the
methods of the Besozzis; and around 1767 he entered the service
of Frederick the Great (1712–88) as successor to Carl Philipp
Emanuel Bach (1714–88). Shortly afterwards he went to
London. In the years that followed he gave concerts all over
Europe, and became the most sought-after oboist of them all. His
*Favourite Concerto for the Hoboy or German Flute with Instrumental
Parts* was very famous and inspired various composers to write
variations, including Wolfgang Amadeus Mozart (1756–91),
who heard Fischer in Holland in 1766 and composed *12
variations for piano on a Mínuet by J.C. Fischer*. (The theme comes
from the finale.)

Johann Zoffany (1734/35–1810): Thomas Gainsborough c 1771/72.

In 1780 he was appointed chamber musician to Queen Charlotte, the wife of George III (1738–1820), and in London he played with the 'London' Bach, Johann Christian (1735–82) and the *viola da gamba* virtuoso Carl Friedrich Abel (1723–87). He was held in high esteem by the aristocracy and married the daughter of the famous painter Thomas Gainsborough (1727–88). In 1800 he died of a stroke while performing before the Royal family.

The shift in the style of playing towards the end of the eighteenth century transpires in a letter from Wolfgang Amadeus Mozart to his father in Salzburg written in 1787.

Ramm and the two Fischers, the bass singer and the oboist from London came here this Lent. If the latter when we knew him in Holland played no better than he does now, he certainly does not deserve the reputation he enjoys. But this is between ourselves. In those days I was not competent to form an opinion. All that I remember is that I liked his playing immensely, as indeed everyone did. This is quite understandable, of course, on the assumption that taste can undergo remarkable changes. Possibly he plays in some old-fashioned style? Not at all! The long and the short of it is that he plays like a bad beginner. Young André, who took some lessons from Fiala, plays a thousand times better. And then his concertos! His own compositions! Why, each ritornello lasts a quarter of an hour; and then our hero comes in, lifts up one leaden foot after the other and stamps on the floor with each turn. His tone is entirely nasal, and his held notes like the tremulant on the organ. Would you ever have thought that his playing is like this? Yet it is nothing but the truth, though a truth which I should only tell to you.

The Letters of Mozart and His Family. Vol. III. Translated and edited by Emily Anderson, London, 1938, pp. 1350–1.

The Bassoon in the Baroque and Pre-Classical Eras

We have seen that the transformation of the shawm into the oboe probably took place in the second half of the seventeenth century, and that from this time on, performance directions occur more frequently. The word 'fagott' (bassoon) had already been used for the old one-piece instrument, which is nowadays normally called dulcian (especially by makers of historical reproductions). As the sound of the dulcian was more adaptable than that of the bass pommer, it tended to be used (and was stipulated) in instrumental works at the beginning of the seventeenth century. Michael Praetorius made use of the bassoon, and Giovanni Gabrieli (1557–1612) wrote for it in his famous *Symphoniae Sacrae*. Gabrieli's pupil Heinrich Schütz (1585–1672) made constant use of the instrument; for example, his 24th Psalm of 1619 requires the following instruments: '2 cornetti, 2 violini, 5 fagotti and 4 tromboni'.

In chamber music written between 1600 and 1650 the bassoon is mainly used as an accompanying basso continuo instrument, but is also given solo passages. Giovanni Antonio Bertoli (fl *c* 1639–45) is one of the first bassoonists whose name is still known to us; in 1645 he published some of his music for the bassoon in a collection entitled *Compositioni Musicali . . . Fatte Per Sonare col fagotto solo*. The C–d' range enables us to deduce that the instrument concerned was a two-keyed dulcian.[48]

Home of the Hotteterre family in La Couture-Boussey.

Makers' marks on Hotteterre instruments.

The first didactic instructions for the bassoon were included in *Grundrichtiger kurtz leicht und nöthiger Unterricht Der musicalischen Kunst* (1687) by Georg Daniel Speer (1636–1707), who also made a name as a Baroque poet. From 1688 to 1690 he was imprisoned on account of a political pamphlet, but at the express permission of the Göppinger magistrate was later able to resume his duties as cantor. Around 1700 the bassoon began to be used as a solo instrument: Antonio Vivaldi (*c* 1678–1741), for example, wrote no less than 38 bassoon concertos. Mozart poked fun at the horn soloist Ignaz Leutgeb (*c* 1745–1811) by writing *Wolfgang Amadé Mozart hat sich über den Leitgeb, Esel, Ochs, und Narr erbarmt zu Wien den 17 May 1783*[49] (Wolfgang Amadé Mozart took pity on Leitgeb, the ass, the ox, and the fool, in Vienna on 17 May 1783), as a dedication in the E flat major horn concerto K417; and Vivaldi did the same in the bassoon concerto P.382 by writing Con^to p. Gioseppino Biancardi o sia fagotto.[50]

Johann Friedrich Lampe (1703–51) was Handel's bassoonist. He studied music at Helmstedt, went to London in 1725 and played at the King's Theatre and in Vauxhall Gardens. Thomas Stanesby junior (1692–1754) is said to have built an early example of a double bassoon for him at the behest of Handel. Yet according to Burney it was not used in the *Hymn for the Coronation* at the coronation of George II (1683–1760) in 1727. Lampe also wrote *A Plain and Compendious Method of Teaching Thorough Bass*, London, 1737.

Instrument Making in the Seventeenth and Eighteenth Centuries

The metamorphosis of the one-part dulcian into the four-part bassoon consisting of wing, butt, long and bell joints took place in stages. The reason it was split up into several parts was probably not because this made the instrument easier to carry, but rather that it was easier to machine the bore of short pieces of wood with great precision. Makers also began to employ more expensive materials such as ebony, boxwood and ivory, all of which had to be imported, in place of native fruitwood, beech and oak.

The claim that the Hotteterres divided and remodelled the body of the shawm and dulcian and thereby produced the oboe and the bassoon seems plausible, for members of the family, which can be traced back to the fourteenth century in the parish of La Couture-Boussey, had been wood turners since the sixteenth century. A number of well-known woodwind instrument makers have their workshops in the village to this day. (The accompanying excerpt from the Hotteterre family tree lists only the most important members of this numerous family.)

In addition to being split up into three parts the oboe was provided with an e flat' key, both on the left and on the right. Thus the player could choose between operating the keys with the little finger of the right hand, as is still done today, or with the little finger of the left hand. The c' key had a fishtailed touchpiece (which continued to be supplied by instrument makers long after the left-hand key had disappeared, no doubt prompted by a feeling for symmetry). Early oboes thus had three keys, whereas later oboes had only two, the latter form surviving into the nineteenth century. The top joint was turned like a baluster at the top end; and that part of the bottom joint into which the tenon of the top joint fitted was strengthened by two raised circular rings or turnings. These were left in place when the oboe was being made, and provided mountings for the keys, which were made of brass. In the case of expensive instruments keys were sometimes made of silver and decorated with engravings.

The bell joint really did look like a bell, and had one or even two

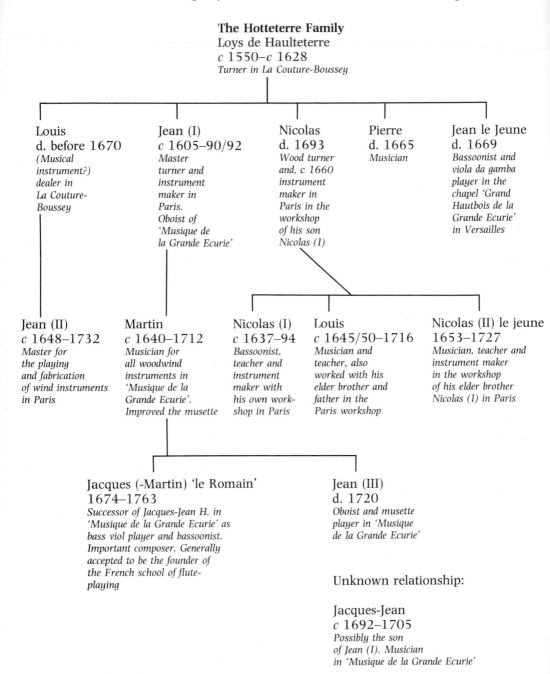

The Hotteterre Family
Loys de Haulteterre
c 1550–c 1628
Turner in La Couture-Boussey

Louis
d. before 1670
(Musical
instrument?)
dealer in
La Couture-
Boussey

Jean (I)
c 1605–90/92
Master
turner and
instrument
maker in
Paris.
Oboist of
'Musique de
la Grande Ecurie'

Nicolas
d. 1693
Wood turner
and, c 1660
instrument
maker in
Paris in the
workshop
of his son
Nicolas (I)

Pierre
d. 1665
Musician

Jean le Jeune
d. 1669
Bassoonist and
viola da gamba
player in the
chapel 'Grand
Hautbois de la
Grande Ecurie'
in Versailles

Jean (II)
c 1648–1732
Master for
the playing
and fabrication
of wind instruments
in Paris

Martin
c 1640–1712
Musician for
all woodwind
instruments in
'Musique de la
Grande Ecurie'.
Improved the musette

Nicolas (I)
c 1637–94
Bassoonist,
teacher and
instrument
maker with
his own work-
shop in Paris

Louis
c 1645/50–1716
Musician and
teacher, also
worked with his
elder brother and
father in the
Paris workshop

Nicolas (II) le jeune
1653–1727
Musician, teacher and
instrument maker
in the workshop
of his elder brother
Nicolas (I) in Paris

Jacques (-Martin) 'le Romain'
1674–1763
Successor of Jacques-Jean H. in
'Musique de la Grande Ecurie' as
bass viol player and bassoonist.
Important composer. Generally
accepted to be the founder of
the French school of flute-
playing

Jean (III)
d. 1720
Oboist and musette
player in 'Musique
de la Grande Ecurie'

Unknown relationship:

Jacques-Jean
c 1692–1705
Possibly the son
of Jean (I). Musician
in 'Musique de la Grande Ecurie'

resonance holes at the top. At the bottom end it was somewhat narrower. The baluster on the top joint was designed to prevent condensation and to stop the instrument from developing cracks. For this reason ivory or horn rings were often added to the top and middle joints and to the bell. A variant of the 'straight top' oboe made only in England eschewed the baluster on the top joint. In fact only the Viennese oboe has retained the baluster and the characteristic bell shape. In the case of the French oboe, which is nowadays found all over the world, the baluster has shrunk to a mere swelling and the bell is only slightly flared. (*See the pictures of the oboes on pages 53, 68–9, 82–3.*)

In the eighteenth century the introduction of new keys received only a guarded welcome. It is true that a surveyor by the name of Gerhard Hoffmann (1690–1757) is said to have invented the a flat' and b flat' keys for the transverse flute as early as 1727, and to have applied his invention to the oboe, but evidently little notice was taken of this, for not long afterwards the Hamburg flautist Peter Nicolas Petersen (1761–1830)[51] also claimed to have made this invention. The court instrument maker Johann Heinrich Wilhelm Grenser (1764–1813) was sceptical about keys, as were many musicians at the end of the eighteenth century.

In 1800 he wrote:

> To add a key in order to improve this note or that is neither difficult nor artful. And then keys are not all that new, for when I was a boy I made use of them in order to bolster up the weak notes, and it became easy to give them their proper place . . .[52]

In 1823 the famous oboe virtuoso Wilhelm Theodor Johann Braun (1796–1867) commented on the use of keys as follows.

German oboes between 1800 and 1860

1. *Anonymous oboe. Boxwood, with nine brass keys, c 1820.*

2. *Anonymous oboe. Boxwood, with 11 silver keys, c 1840.*

3. *Johann Adam Heckel (1812–77), Biebrich. Boxwood oboe with 11 brass keys, c 1850.*

4. *Eberhard Wünnenberg (1812–77), Cologne. Boxwood oboe with 13 brass keys, c 1850.*

5. *Berthold & Söhne (1849–92), Speyer. Boxwood oboe with 13 German silver keys, c 1860.*

(Gunther Joppig Collection.) Photo: Frehn.

German oboes with German silver keys from c 1870–1900

1. *Anonymous Viennese oboe with 13 keys, c 1870.*

2. *A.E. Fischer (firm founded 1864), Bremen. Grenadilla oboe with 14 keys, c 1880.*

3. *Oskar Oehler (1858–1936), Berlin. Cocus-wood oboe with 13 keys, c 1890.*

4. *Vinzenz Püchner (d. 1948), Graslitz. Cocus-wood oboe with 11 German silver keys, c 1900.*

5. *Heckel (firm founded 1831), Biebrich. Grenadilla oboe with 12 German silver keys, c 1900.*

(Gunther Joppig Collection.) Photo: Frehn.

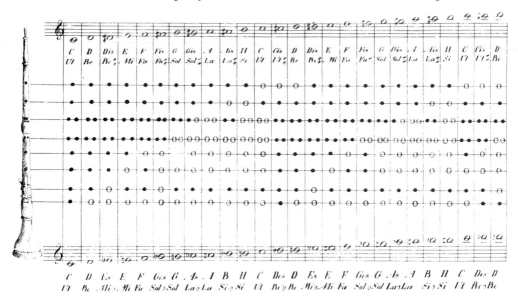

Fingering chart for the classical two-keyed oboe, c 1800.

Too many keys would seem to impair the tone; and they have the added disadvantage that if they are imperfectly made one soon finds that the one or the other does not cover the holes properly. The advantages do not outweigh the attendant disadvantages.[52]

The transformation of the dulcian took place in a number of stages. A two-part instrument is mentioned by the scholar Marin Mersenne (1588–1648) in his *Harmonie Universelle* of 1636/37, which includes a picture of a bassoon. An interesting piece of corroborative evidence for a two-part dulcian is instrument no. 200 on plate XXXVIII in the catalogue of the Vienna collection.[53] Wing and long joints are still in one piece, being inserted into the butt joint. Not long after this the instrument became tripartite, and the wing joint was separated from the long joint. The extension from C to low B flat finally made the long joint so lengthy that it became necessary to divide it into a real long joint and a bell joint.

A divided long joint has now been developed which makes it possible to accommodate the bassoon in a fairly small case. An instrument of this kind is shown on page 91 (fig. 6). The dulcian had only two keys – the F key, which had a fishtailed touchpiece, and a thumb key for E where there was a thumb hole for D, or a thumb key for D where there was a thumb hole for E. In the first

70

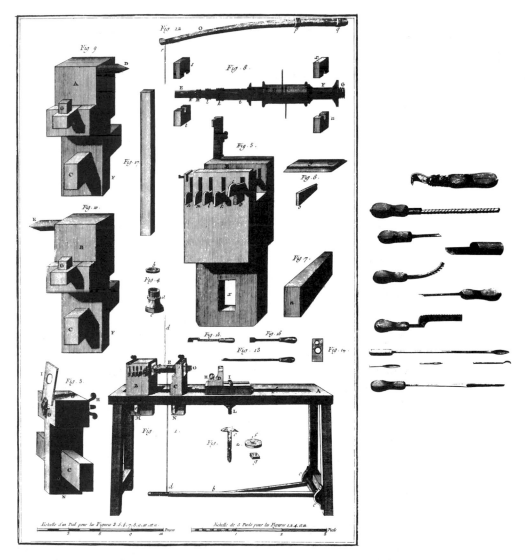

From top to bottom: scraper, straight file, burin, bent file, awl, saw and various flat and spoon bits.

Lathe and tools of an eighteenth-century woodwind instrument maker. From Denis Diderot's Encylopédie. *Briasson edition 1751–72.*

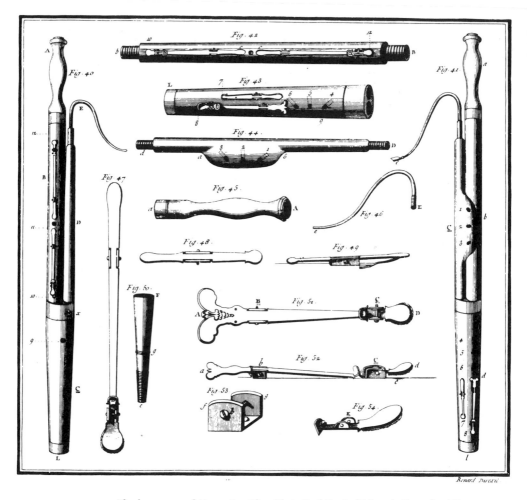

The bassoon and its parts. After Plate 9 of Denis Diderot's Encyclopédie. *Briasson edition 1751–72.*

case the key is below, in the second case above the thumb hole. The remodelled four-joint bassoon (not including the crook) had keys for F, D and C in the lower octave. Bassoons with four keys had an additional G sharp key. In this way the right hand below left hand posture finally became the rule. The practice of fitting the F key with a fishtailed touchpiece continued right up to the beginning of the nineteenth century. Evidence of this is provided by a bassoon in the Heckel collection by F.G.A. Kirst, Potsdam, which is dated 1801.[54]

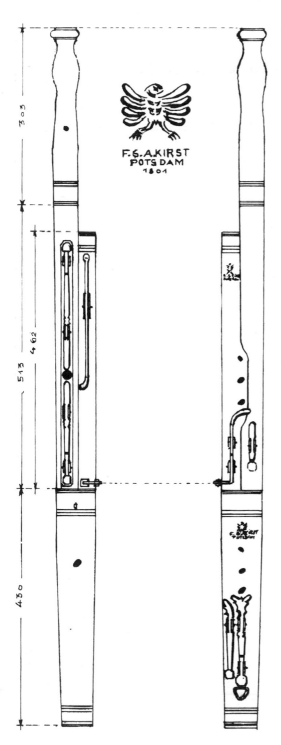

Drawing of a bassoon by Friedrich Gabriel August Kirst, c 1750–1806. (Heckel Museum, Wiesbaden-Biebrich.)

FIVE

The Later Development of the Oboe and the Bassoon

At the end of the eighteenth and at the beginning of the nineteenth centuries the classical instruments – the flute, the oboe, the clarinet and the bassoon – usually had no more than two keys. The transverse flute had a C sharp key and the clarinet a' and b flat' keys. In the case of the clarinet, however, the decisive improvement had already been made. This was the introduction of the long E key, which made it possible by means of overblowing to reach b', and of the long F sharp key. From 1750 onwards transverse flutes descending to low c' began to be made, i.e. the makers supplied an additional foot joint which had c sharp' and c' keys in addition to the d sharp key. These improvements began to be transferred to other wind instruments. The G sharp and F keys, which had been in use on the bassoon for some time, were joined by the B flat key.

Around 1810 many players still tended to prefer the two-key oboe, though there were already instruments in existence which had five, six and even eight keys. The ancient practice of playing semitones by means of cross-fingering and closing lower tone holes thus began to lose its validity. After a semitone key had been fitted it became clear that the tone of this note differed markedly from that previously achieved by means of cross-fingering, and players were suddenly no longer satisfied with the other notes. But that was only one aspect of these experiments with keys, which continued to be carried out on old instruments until improvements became noticeable.

The beginning of the nineteenth century was also an age that entertained a firm belief in progress, and it was the time of the first significant scientific research in acoustics. Ernst Florens Friedrich Chladni (1759–1827) devoted several chapters of his book *Die Akustik* (Leipzig, 1802) to wind instruments, to the acoustics of open and stopped pipes and to the right acoustic placing of tone holes. The flautist Johann Georg Tromlitz (1725–1805) had

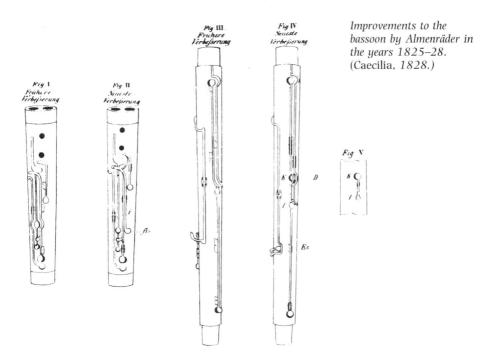

Fig III
Frühere
Verbesserung

Fig IV
Neueste
Verbesserung

*Improvements to the bassoon by Almenräder in the years 1825–28.
(Caecilia, 1828.)*

Fig I
Frühere
Verbesserung

Fig II
Neueste
Verbesserung

Fig V

started the debate prior to this with an article, *Über die Flöten mit mehreren Klappen* (Concerning flutes with several keys), published in 1800 in the *Allgemeine musikalische Zeitung.*

These problems were hotly debated by the specialists, and led to some heated exchanges in learned journals. (We had occasion to quote Heinrich Grenser on the subject in the previous chapter.) Tromlitz belonged to a generation of players who were extremely good practical musicians in addition to being skilled instrument makers, and who were thus able to present their improvements in a convincing way to a critical specialist public. Musicians are, on the whole, of a conservative disposition, and if they have once learnt an instrument they are rarely prepared to adapt themselves to a new system.

Karl Almenräder (1786–1843) was one of a number of talented bassoonists who were also good instrument makers. While he was in Cologne (1820–22) he set up a woodwind instrument manufacturing business, and in 1820 he published the *Abhandlung über die Verbesserung des Fagotts* (Treatise concerning the improvement of the bassoon). Almenräder was a close friend of Gottfried Weber (1779–1839), who also published a number of articles on this subject, including a *Versuch einer praktischen Akustik der Blasinstrumente* (Essay on the practical

75

The Later Development of the Oboe and the Bassoon

Eighteenth and nineteenth century bassoons

1. *Dutch racket by W. Wyne, Nijmegen, c 1700. Musikinstrumentenmuseum, Berlin.*

2. *English bassoon by Wrede (workshop dates 1810–49), London, with six keys. Photo: Sotheby's.*

3. *French tenoroon (fagottino) by Jean-Nicholas Savary (1786–1850), Paris, with ten keys. Photo: Sotheby's.*

4. *German bassoon by G. Zencker jun. (1786–1848), Adorf, with eight keys, c 1810.*

5. *'Dresden' bassoon by Grenser & Wiesner (1791–1868), Dresden with 17 keys, c 1840.*

6. *Two wing joints of differing length for the Grenser & Wiesner bassoon.*

(4–6 Gunther Joppig Collection.) Photo: Frehn.

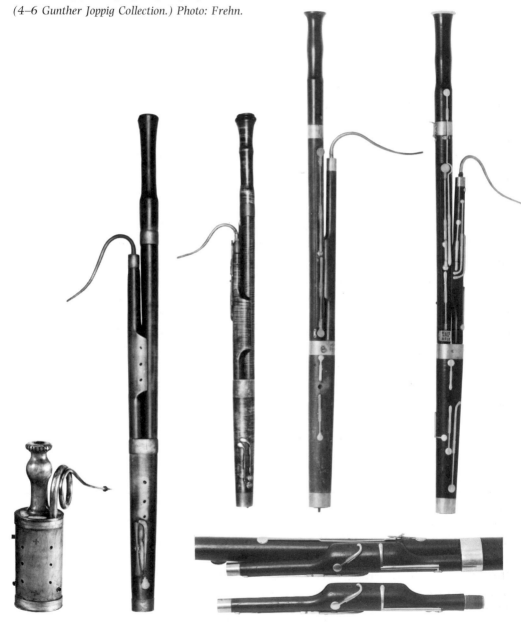

acoustics of wind instruments). Weber was the editor of a new periodical, *Caecilia*, and in 1825 he devoted considerable space to Karl Almenräder's suggestions in a review entitled *Wesentliche Verbesserungen des Fagotts* (Considerable improvements to the bassoon).

Improvements were also being made in the case of the clarinet. Here we must mention in particular Iwan Müller (1786–1854), whose *Méthode pour la nouvelle Clarinette et Clarinette-Alto* was published in 1825. (It appeared the same year in German translation in Leipzig.) Iwan Müller presented to a Parisian jury a clarinet with 13 keys that was designed to obviate the necessity of the various tunings. The new B flat clarinet was able to play in all keys with equal facility. The jury's report was not in favour of Müller's innovations, though the process which he had initiated could not be stopped. The novel aspect of his invention was the development of a new kind of key whose leather pads filled with felt were designed to cover the holes more precisely. This came to be of great importance for all other woodwind instruments.

Finally there was the goldsmith and flautist Theobald Boehm (1794–1881), who conducted acoustic experiments with the chemist Karl Franz Emil Schafhäutl (1803–90). In 1833 Schafhäutl published his results in an essay, *Theorie gedackter zylindrischer und konischer Pfeifen und Querflöten* (Theory of stopped cylindrical and conical pipes and transverse flutes). In 1832 Theobald Boehm revealed a completely redesigned transverse flute, the conical flute. He altered the instrument in a radical manner, dividing up its body and boring the holes in accordance with the results of his acoustic research, and then tried to develop a practical system of fingering for the keys. In all this the profound knowledge of precision engineering that he had acquired in the Swiss clockmaking industry proved to be very useful.

Instruments by Adolphe Sax.
1. Boehm system bassoon
2. Conical flute 1844
3. and 4. Tenor and baritone saxophones
c 1848

1

2

3

4

E.F.F. Chladni (1759–1827)

There were of course many other inventors, whose number can best be gauged by looking through old collections of patents. People plagiarized, copied and laid claim to inventions to an extent which would warrant a book in itself. (Only the most important innovators have been mentioned here.) They were later joined by Adolphe Sax (1814–94), who also revolutionized instrument making. The men mentioned up to this point had one thing in common – in addition to being talented inventors they were all outstanding musicians who were able to demonstrate convincingly the possibilites inherent in their new instruments. It was this fact that led colleagues, composers and critics to think

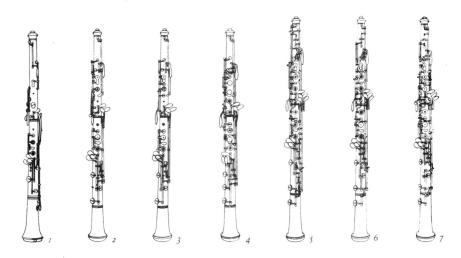

Triébert family instruments
1. Triébert System No. 3
(1840)
2. Triébert System No. 4
(1843)

3. Triébert System No. 5
(1849)
4. Boehm System (1860)
5. Barret System (1862)

6. Triébert System No. 6
(1875)
7. Gillet System (1882)

about improvements, to discuss them and finally to accept them, albeit initially in a rather half-hearted manner.

Let us now pursue the history of the oboe and the bassoon separately, for the earlier similarities with regard to fingering now come to an end. Whereas in the eighteenth century there were many musicians who could play both the oboe and the bassoon, increasing mechanization meant that the two instruments drifted further and further apart, with the result that it became increasingly difficult to play both. Specialization became the rule, particularly as the demands made on the players continued to increase, and because regular orchestras came into being in which one musician was employed for every instrument. Someone who could play everything, such as the medieval jongleur, and later the town piper, was thus no longer in demand. Only in the field of military music did the kind of musician survive who had to be able to play both a wind and a string instrument in order to fulfil the various duties assigned to him.

In France Henri Brod (1799–1839) not only made and improved instruments, but also had a decisive influence on the training of oboists with his *Méthode pour le Hautbois*, which was published in Paris around 1826. In the meantime another family of instrument makers had established itself in the French capital – the Triéberts. The head of the family, Georges-Louis-Guillaume (Wilhelm) Triébert (1770–1848) moved from Storndorf in Hessen to Paris, where he began to make oboes. His son, Fréderic Triébert (1813–78), was to the oboe what Theobald Boehm was to the Boehm flute, developing the so-called 'French oboe', the successors of which we are to all intents and purposes still playing today. The elder Triébert brought many of his ideas on oboe construction from Germany, where a type of oboe with eight to ten keys was already in existence. It was for this instrument that the oboist Josef Sellner (1787–1843) produced a tutor as early as 1825 which has lost practically none of its significance.

Yet in Germany the French methods have never really managed to make much headway, and generations of oboists have studied on the basis of the Rosenthal tutor, which appeared in 1908. Triébert narrowed the bore of the oboe even further, and since then it has been possible to speak of a French and a German bore. With regard to the keywork, cherished traditions which had primarily been influenced by instrument makers who

Staccato run up to f''' from the Adagio and Polonaise.

Joseph Panny (1794–1838)

considered themselves first and foremost to be wood turners and not precision engineers were jettisoned. Makers began to discard superfluous ornamentation and to adopt ways of mounting the keys which had in the meantime proved their worth. Thus, for example, the instrument maker Laurent had developed glass flutes in Paris as early as 1806. These of course had no ornamental turnings, and for this reason alone he was forced to

Typical Viennese oboe from c 1930 by Hermann Zuleger (1885–1949) (Joppig Collection; Photo Reiberger)

make use of a new kind of key mounting. This was the origin of 'pillar' mountings. Louis-Auguste Buffet's needle springs and Theobald Boehm's open keys were also incorporated in the design, and so within a space of three decades six different models appeared, versions of which are still in use today. The thumbplate system roughly corresponds to system no. 5, whereas system no. 6 is the open key oboe still in use today. (*See illustration p. 83, nos. 1 and 3.*)

In view of the growing number of performances of early music which make use of old instruments or modern reproductions, one asks oneself why an instrument that is as complicated as the oboe was ever developed at all. The answer would be that each minute alteration in the bore of the tone holes and the body led to far-reaching consequences. (To this day the acoustics of the oboe and the bassoon are inadequately understood.) The introduction of keys made it imperative to provide keys for more and more tone holes. In the case of the flute the Boehm system has led to a situation where none of the tone holes are covered directly by the fingers. In that of the clarinet and the bassoon certain tone holes for some of the notes of the basic scale are still covered directly, yet even here the use of keys has increased. The introduction of speaker keys – in the case of the oboe there are now three of these – was a logical result of the greater number of keys which, together with the changes in the bore, had led to a deterioration in the response of the notes in the upper octaves.

An American who compared the acoustics of the French oboe with those of the improved German oboe (which is still played today by the oboists of the Vienna Philharmonic) showed that on the whole the 'Viennese' oboe responds more readily than the French instrument. Originally there were no octave keys and yet, as the literature amply illustrates, oboists played up to f‴ nonetheless. Instances of this can be found in Beethoven's *Fidelio*,

Belgian and French oboes

1. Couesnon & Cie (from 1882 successors to Gautrot and Triébert), Paris. Musette in F made of boxwood, with six German silver keys, c 1900.

2. Buffet-Crampon (founded 1836), Paris. Boehm system oboe made of grenadilla with 13 German silver keys, c 1870. (Trade mark Weril.)

3.and 4. Charles Mahillon (1813–87), Brussels. Rosewood oboe with 15 German silver keys based on Triébert systems no. 4 and 5, c 1880.

5. Jacques Albert (founded 1846), Brussels. Rosewood oboe with 16 German silver keys based on the Barret system c 1920.

(Gunther Joppig Collection.) Photo: Frehn.

Modern twentieth century oboes

1. Gebrüder Mönnig, Markneukirchen. Plexiglass oboe with 18 German silver keys based on the Conservatoire system (no. 6).

2. Georg Urban (d. 1965), Hamburg. Boxwood oboe with 20 silver keys based on the compromise system, which enables both German and French fingering to be used, c 1930.

3. Heckel (founded 1831), Biebrich. Grenadilla oboe no. 35, 1966.

4. Oscar Adler (founded 1885), Markneukirchen. Grenadilla oboe with 24 German silver keys based on Gillet's Plateaux system. 1973.

(Gunther Joppig Collection.) Photo: Frehn.

Mozart's Oboe Quartet, in the quartets of Joseph Fiala (*c* 1754–1816), and in the *Adagio and Polonaise* by Joseph Panny (1794–1838), a virtuoso piece for solo oboe, solo bassoon and orchestra.

Throughout the nineteenth century there were two kinds of oboe: the French model, which became the rule in the Romance countries and also in Britain; and the German oboe, which continued to be played in Germany and Austria. Naturally the German makers gradually adopted the improvements in keywork. Instead of brass they made increasing use of German silver, and in addition to this keys mounted on turnings were discarded in favour of 'pillar' mountings. The baluster (or 'onion-head') could now be withdrawn, and particularly good instruments were given exchangeable finials or even exchangeable top joints of differing lengths, so-called *corps de rechange*.

Yet even in Germany the French oboe gradually won the day. Writers on instruments and on orchestration now began to compare the German oboe with the French oboe – and the comparison was unfavourable for the German oboe. Around 1920 the German oboist Fritz Flemming (1873–1947) finally introduced the French oboe both in the orchestra and at the Berlin Conservatory. Many instrument makers now began to combine the old German system of fingering with the bore of the French instrument in order to improve the tonal qualities of the German oboe. The resistance to this should not be underestimated, particularly in the case of those oboists who had studied the German system in their youth. The Hamburg instrument maker Georg Urban even developed a 'compromise system' which enabled the oboist to use both systems of fingering and meant that he was able to adapt slowly to the French system. (An instrument of this kind is depicted on page 83, no. 2.)

The success of the Boehm flute led to repeated attempts by instrument makers to transfer the Boehm system to the oboe.

Saxophone-fingering oboe by Louis Musical Instrument Company, London, about 1930, with single-reed mouthpiece (Joppig Collection; photo Söffke, Hamburg)

Boehm himself left calculations on how to do this and in fact made a handful of such instruments. Karl Ventzke's book *Boehm-Oboen und die neueren französischen Oboensysteme* gives an exhaustive account of these constructions. The so-called Berninger oboe on the other hand had a mouthpiece with a small single reed, which meant that the player only had to make single reeds instead of the more complicated double reeds. In other words, the Berninger oboe had the *embouchure* of the clarinet. Although the quality of the tone was only imperceptibly affected, hardly anyone was convinced of the necessity of this innovation, and so this proved to be another of those instruments that had to be consigned to the inventor's lumber room.

Old advertisements show that the English firm of Boosey & Hawkes once sold an oboe with saxophone fingering; in other words, using the modified Boehm system. Early instruments of this kind were made by the Louis Musical Instrument Company, which was founded in London in 1923. There have been repeated attempts to produce smaller oboes – the musette (*see p. 82, no. 1*) is an example of this. Yet this instrument has only been used in folk music. For some time it was a favourite instrument of amateurs, similar in this respect to the flageolet. The piccolo heckelphone in F and the heckelphone in E flat never progressed beyond the prototype stage. The bore of these instruments is very wide, as in the case of the large heckelphone, and for this reason the tone was very much like that of a shawm. Yet, as the author's attempts to play them shows, a model with perfect intonation never materialized, and thus the firm soon stopped making them. They were only used on a few occasions, one of them being a performance of the second Brandenburg Concerto in an arrangement by Philipp Wolfrum (1854–1919) where the piccolo heckelphone took the part of the high solo trumpet, at times playing in unison with two clarinets in C. What this sounded like is left to the reader's imagination. The conductor was none other than Richard Strauss (1864–1949), who, as is shown by entries in the visitors' book, was in close touch with the firm of Heckel.

The development of the bassoon actually happened the other way round if we look at it from a national angle. For whereas the French, strictly speaking, retained the old bassoon and simply added more keys to it – to this day the instrument they refer to as basson does not have an E key – Karl Almenräder began to subject the bassoon to a thorough overhaul. It was a stroke of luck that when he became court musician in Biebrich he also undertook to supervise the manufacturing of woodwind instruments for the famous music publishing firm of B. Schott's Söhne, which had been founded by Bernhard Schott (1748–1809) in Mainz in 1770, and which at this time still made instruments.

In 1829 a talented 17-year-old instrument maker called Johann Adam Heckel (1812–77), who had learned his craft from relatives in the Vogtland in Saxony, entered the firm. Almenräder no doubt noticed the young man's unique talent and abilities at once. On 11 March 1831 the two of them founded their own firm, which proposed to devote itself to the exploitation of Almenräder's improvements to the bassoon. Now this was not at all easy, for at the time there were numerous firms making bassoons, some of which will be mentioned at this juncture. There was the Grenser workshop in Dresden, whose Dresden bassoons had an excellent reputation. (A Grenser & Wiesner bassoon is depicted on page 76, nos. 5 and 6. It has wing joints of differing lengths [*corps de rechange*] and already possesses 17 keys.) Further important firms were Haseneier in Koblenz and Uhlmann in Vienna. In France Savary instruments had an excellent reputation; and of course the Triéberts also made bassoons.

In the early days – until its own brand name became

sufficiently well known – Heckel probably made some instruments for Schott, which were stamped with the latter's maker's mark. The reputation of the famous bassoonist Karl Almenräder no doubt helped to ensure the success of the new venture. It is true that all kinds of woodwind instruments were made at the Heckel workshops, yet particular emphasis was placed on the bassoon, which was especially difficult to make – a lot of time and work had to be invested in a good model. Heckel also made and improved the double bassoon. In a very short space of time the firm had acquired an enviable reputation. After the death of Almenräder the business was carried on by Johann Adam Heckel and his son Wilhelm Heckel (1856–1909), who were both intent on improving the instrument.

The opinion of composers was sought at an early stage, and Richard Wagner (1813–83), who lived in Biebrich in 1862 while working on the *Meistersinger*, was a frequent guest at the Heckel workshops. It is said that he once tried to turn a piece of wood, which sprang out of the lathe because he took insufficient care. (A scene in *Meistersinger* is said to have been inspired by this incident.) Wagner subsequently showed his liking for Heckel instruments by recommending them to others. In 1879 he was shown a completely redesigned and newly developed double bassoon, which was unanimously praised by the experts. Up to that time double bassoons had been unwieldy instruments which were unbalanced both with regard to tone and intonation, and thus of limited use in symphony orchestras. Wilhelm Heckel and his two sons managed to perfect the shape that the instrument has retained to this day.

In 1889 Wilhelm Heckel patented one of the most important inventions in the history of the bassoon – the rubber lining of the wing and butt joints. These parts of the instrument were particularly affected by condensation, and musicians had to take

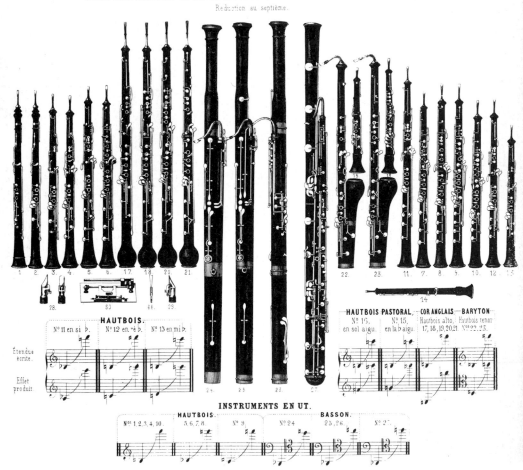

Prospectus for the Triébert firm in 1855, when Guillaume Triébert was Chairman.

Johann Adam Heckel (1812–77), the founder of the firm that bears his name.

Workbench of a Heckel instrument maker, c 1920.

Makers' Marks

1831
B. SCHOTT FILS A MAYENCE.

Until 1845
HECKEL BIEBRICH

1877
HECKEL BIEBRICH
SYSTEM. F. STRITTER.

c 1900
HECKEL BIEBRICH
SOLE AGENTS
COOPER & LLOYD
12 SNOW HILL WOLVERHAMPTON

1914
HECKEL BIEBRICH

HECKELPHON

The Wagner villa on the banks of the Rhine at Biebrich, which was built by the architect Wilhelm Frickhöfer. Richard Wagner lived here in 1862.

great care to ensure that the wood did not perish. The rubber lining finally solved the problem. At about the same time the connecting U-tube between the twin bores in the butt joint was redesigned. Originally they had been joined by a slide, but this was replaced by a water cap held in place by screws. By the turn of the century the firm of Heckel had manufactured about 3000 bassoons in addition to about 1000 other woodwind instruments.

If one disregards certain minor modifications to the bore and the keys, there have to this day been no significant changes in the Heckel bassoon, and if one compares a turn-of-the-century bassoon with a modern instrument, it may be surprising to note that the keywork is the same today as it was 80 years ago. Bassoonists have profited most of all from this tradition, and it has led to the use of the Heckel bassoon all over the world. At the turn of the century the firm's competitors were already advertising their products by stating that they were based on the Heckel

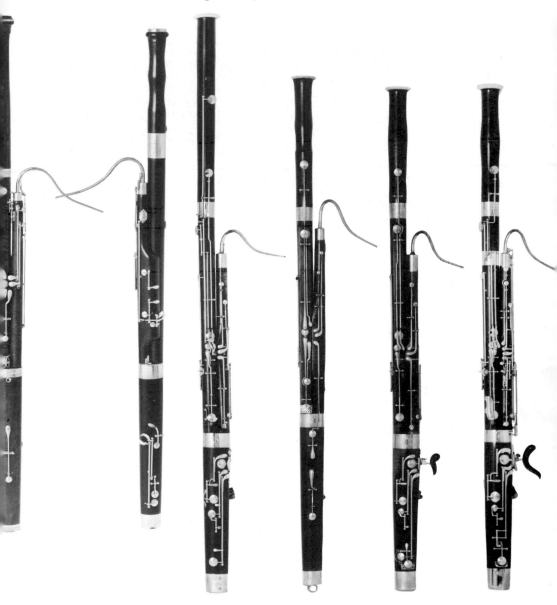

Various forms of the bassoon in the last hundred years

1. French bassoon by Gautrot (workshop dates 1845–84), Paris, c 1870. From the Manaus Opera on the Amazon in Brazil.

2. Bassoon made wholly of ebonite, no maker's mark, English origin, c 1920.

3. German Heckel-system bassoon by Reinhold Lange (1854–1905), Wiesbaden, with Wagner bell for the low A, c 1900.

4. Austrian bassoon by Karl Stecher (1820–1904), Vienna, c 1880.

5. Heckel bassoon with moulding on the long joint, No. 4269, made in 1902.

6. Heckel bassoon with divided long joint, No. 12394, made in 1979.

(Gunther Joppig Collection.) Photo: Frehn.

Views of the Heckel workshop in Wiesbaden-Biebrich, c 1920. The drills and lathes are still belt-driven today.

model. In fact, they paid them the ultimate compliment by making exact copies.

In France, on the other hand, there has been no significant remodelling of the bassoon since the beginning of the nineteenth century, especially with regard to the bore and the tone quality. True, the number of keys on these bassoons also increased, but to all intents and purposes the old bassoon remained unaltered. It has on the whole a more humming and marked tone, which has the disadvantage, perhaps, that in chords it does not blend as well with the other instruments as does the Heckel bassoon.

Around the world the German bassoon continued to gain ground. In Britain the decision to adopt this model was taken in the 1920s; and in the United States it is now also the prevalent instrument. The French model predominates only in the Ro-

92

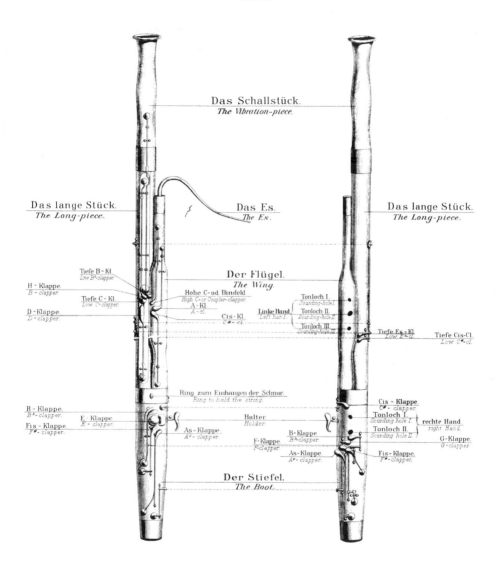

Das Schallstück.
The Vibration-piece.

Das lange Stück.
The Long-piece.

Das Es.
The Es.

Das lange Stück.
The Long-piece.

Der Flügel.
The Wing.

Tiefe B - Kl.
Low B♭ clapper.

H - Klappe.
B - clapper.

Tiefe C - Kl.
Low C♯ clapper.

Hohe C - od. Bindekl.
High C or Coupler-clapper.

A - Kl.
A - cl.

D - Klappe.
D - clapper.

Cis - Kl.
C♯ - cl.

Linke Hand.
Left hand.

Tonloch I.
Sounding-hole I.

Tonloch II.
Sounding-hole II.

Tonloch III.
Sounding-hole III.

Tiefe Es - Kl.
Low E♭ - cl.

Tiefe Cis-Cl.
Low C♯-cl.

Ring zum Einhangen der Schnur.
Ring to hold the string.

B - Klappe.
B♭ - clapper.

E - Klappe.
E - clapper.

Fis - Klappe.
F♯ - clapper.

As - Klappe.
A♭ - clapper.

Halter
Holder.

F - Klappe.
F - clapper.

B - Klappe.
B♭ clapper.

As - Klappe.
A♭ - clapper.

Cis - Klappe.
C♯ - clapper.

Tonloch I.
Sounding hole I.

Tonloch II.
Sounding hole II.

rechte Hand.
right Hand.

Fis - Klappe.
F♯ - clapper.

G - Klappe.
G - clapper.

Der Stiefel.
The Boot.

Der Fagott
The Bassoon
und
and
die Benennung seiner Theile und Klappen.
the names of its parts and clappers.

Fagott.
Modell 1883 aus der Fabrik
von W. Heckel. Königl.
Hofinstrumentenmacher;
Biebrich °/ Rhein.

'Tafel I' from the first edition of the famous bassoon-tutor of Christian Julius Weissenborn (1837–1888), Leipzig 1887, page 155.

mance countries, in parts of Canada and in South America. In the nineteenth century there were many firms that made French bassoons. They included Gautrot, who developed the sarrusophones; Adolphe Sax; and, also in Belgium, the firm of Mahillon. Today there are really only two firms, Buffet-Crampon and Selmer, which manufacture the basson.

The fingering on the French bassoon is considerably different, especially with regard to the long joint, and it requires some getting used to when changing from one system to the other. Recently two French bassoonists have changed instruments, partly under pressure from those guest conductors at the Paris Opéra who conceive of bassoon tone in terms of the Heckel model. The prospects for French bassoonists are not particularly good, for at French conservatories they can only learn the French bassoon. But specializing on this instrument usually prevents them from accepting invitations to play in countries where the German bassoon prevails.

In the case of clarinettists it is the other way round, for the Boehm system clarinet and the bore associated with it has become the norm everywhere except in Germany and Austria, where the clarinet based on the system of Oskar Oehler (1858–1936) continues to be used. In any case it is a deplorable, though possibly inevitable consequence of our media-dominated age that radio, records and television have obscured the salient differences. As a result the national idiosyncracies in orchestral sound seem doomed to disappear.

SIX

Related Instruments

The Oboe d'Amore

Towards the end of the Baroque era the number of instruments in common use declined. In fact whole families vanished and fell into disuse, particularly plucked instruments such as the cittern, chitarrone, lute and guitar, and certain branches of the violin and recorder families. With regard to double reed instruments, by the middle of the eighteenth century their number had virtually been reduced to the oboe in the soprano register and the bassoon in the bass-tenor register.

The principle of families of instruments, which still obtained in the music of the Renaissance, was now discarded completely. Whereas previously the emphasis had been on music for more or less arbitrary instrumental groups, in which precise scoring indications were the exception rather than the rule, there now arose a musical style which stressed the single line and thus the individual instrument. Progress in instrument making and in playing technique meant that the original range of about an octave and a half was considerably extended, and as the ranges of the bassoon and the oboe had reached each other, the intermediate instruments became superfluous. In consort playing it had been important for the various members of a group to produce a homogeneous sound. Now individual sonorities began to be favoured. The oboe and the bassoon in their improved forms survived from among the plethora of pommers, dulcians, sorduns, rackets and crumhorns, though certain members of the various families continued to be used on a regional basis or in certain musical genres.

One of the most sympathetic representatives of the oboe group is the oboe d'amore. It shares its attribute, *d'amore*, with a series of other instruments which were retained in the Baroque era on account of their pleasing sound. The soft tone of the viola d'amore and the violin d'amore, which is reminiscent of the music of the

The beginning of the duet with two obbligato oboes d'amore, 'Herr, dein Mitleid, dein Erbarmen' from the Christmas Oratorio *in the handwriting of Johann Sebastian Bach (1685–1750).*

spheres, is due to freely vibrating sympathetic strings. In wind instruments the distinguishing feature is the bell. This so-called *Liebesfuss* (i.e. love foot) tends only to influence the tonal quality of the lowest notes, and a far more important role is played by the size of the reed and the crook. Originally there was a *d'amore* version of every woodwind instrument. For example, Johann Christian Bach's (1735–82) *Themistocle* requires two clarinets d'amore. There is also evidence that there was a flûte d'amour and a bassoon d'amore, though neither of these instruments has been revived.

The fate of the oboe d'amore was different. After the death of Johann Sebastian Bach the instrument quickly fell into disuse and was almost forgotten; as early as 1800 many writers on music only knew of its existence by hearsay. At this time there originated the commonly repeated assertion that the oboe d'amore was invented around 1720. Yet apart from evidence in the shape of old instruments made before 1720, the extended solo passages in early Bach cantatas point to a widespread use of the instrument at the beginning of the eighteenth century, particularly in northern Germany. It is noticeable that its use was evidently restricted to Protestant church music, to North German Baroque opera, to chamber music and to a handful of solo concertos.

George Frideric Handel, who added a number of concertos and sonatas to the oboe repertoire (he played the oboe in his youth), did not write for the oboe d'amore or the other lower forms of the oboe such as the *taille* or the tenor oboe. Perhaps he did not have

*Mural from a Theban grave of the eighteenth dynasty, second period (1436–
1364 BC). Female musicians and dancers are seen playing and dancing at the
'Beautiful Feast of the Desert Valley' in honour of the dead. The front view,
which is rarely found in Egyptian art, makes it possible to see clearly the reeds of
the double oboe. (British Museum, London, 37 984.) Photo: Hirmer.*

Above: Detail from the Dionysus Mosaic in Cologne (AD 200). A family of satyrs. The maenad on the left is playing a sophisticated double aulos. (Römisch-Germanisches Museum, Cologne.)

Opposite page: Miniatures from the Paris manuscript Ms. lat. 1118 (end of tenth century).

Left: A double shawm.

Right: A jongleur with single shawm. (Bibliothèque Nationale, Paris.)

Below: Miniature from a manuscript of Le Roman d'Alexandre, c.1340 (Ms. Bodley 264) showing a medieval shawm (left) and two long trumpets (right). (Bodleian Library, Oxford.)

Que la cite li rende z fonde ton estage
z te pende a ta porte uoiant tout ton bar

The so-called 'Musicians' Hell' by Hieronymus Bosch (c. 1450–1516). Excerpt from the triptych 'The Garden of Lust' (Prado, Madrid). In hell musicians are condemned to be joined eternally to the instruments with which they spent their sinful lives. The larger-than-life musical instruments, which are depicted with amazing accuracy, become instruments of torture. A pommer forms the diagonal; its pirouette and double reed are clearly visible. A spare reed is seen hanging on a piece of string. The hellish music includes a hurdy-gurdy, a harp, a lute, a fife, a trumpet, a horn, a triangle, a drum and a choir.

One of the oldest and at the same time most beautiful oboes. The real maker's mark, a pennant, has been overstamped by W. Beukers (c.1669–1750). Two oboists, a bassoonist and a tenor oboe player are shown standing around a quartet table (below).

Dancing scene (right). The style of the clothes suggests that the instrument was made in Holland between 1690 and 1700. (Victoria and Albert Museum, London.)

'Pipemaker' by Martin Engelbrecht from 'Assemblage nouveau des manouvries habilles', a series of engravings of artists, craftsmen and professions clad in their own products and tools. Augsburg, c.1730–40

1 *Workbench* 2 *Wood shavings* 3 *Axe* 4 *Drill* 5 *Saw* 6 *Oboe*
7 *Bassoon* 8 and 9 *Cornetts* 10 *Various flutes*

'Female pipemaker' 1 Bagpipes 2 Recorder 3 Bassoon 4 Drill
5 Shawm 6 Chisel 7 Various flutes 8 Cornett 9 Hunting horn
10 Axe 11 Saw 12 Turkish horn

These two prints, which are of the greatest rarity, are reproduced here by kind
permission of Ernst W. Buser, Binningen.

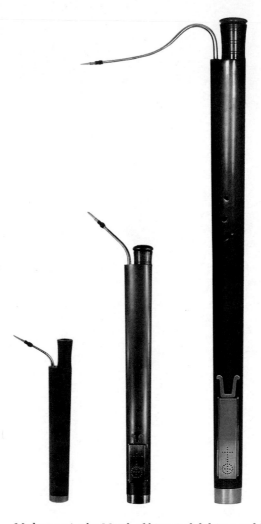

Modern copies by Moeck of historical dulcians and Baroque bassoons.
1 Soprano dulcian
2 Alto dulcian
3 Bass dulcian

4 and 5 Baroque bassoons

Anonymous painting from the first half of the eighteenth century of an unknown oboist with a two-keyed oboe, probably of German origin. The manuscript shows the beginning of a Concerto for Oboe in F minor; a key that, though it posed difficulties for the player, was sometimes used for oboe music at the time, e.g. the concerto in F minor for oboe, strings and basso continuo by Georg Philipp Telemann (1681–1767). (Staatliches Institut für Musikforschung, Berlin.)

'The Bassoonist' by Harmen Hals (1611–69). The musician seems to be on the point of taking a pinch of snuff. The bassoon has the mouldings typical of the Baroque bassoon; its crook, reed and the low C key on the long joint are depicted in great detail. (Suermondt Museum, Aachen.) Photo: Herzog.

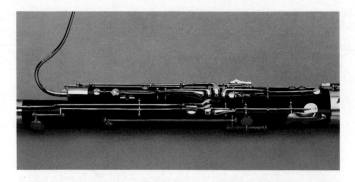

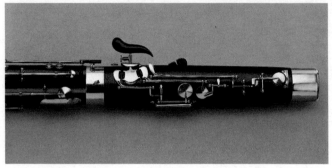

Top: Keys for the left thumb on the modern bassoon.
Above: Keys for the right thumb on the modern bassoon.

Modern double bassoon and bassoons made by W. Schreiber & Söhne, Nauheim. (Works photo.)

'Johann Christian Fischer' by Thomas Gainsborough (1727–88). His two-key boxwood oboe is lying on a Merlin (London) harpsichord-cum-fortepiano. There is a viola on the chair in the background. The picture was painted between 1774 and 1788. (Reproduced by gracious permission of Her Majesty the Queen.)

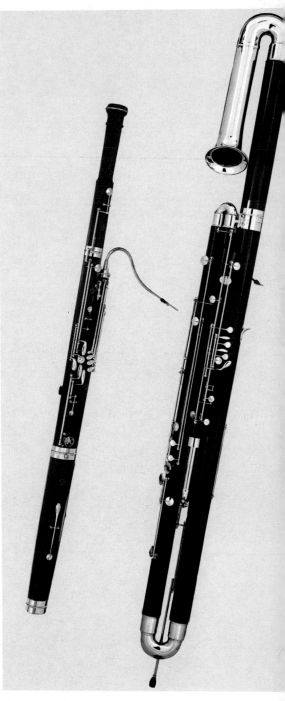

Left: *Modern Heckel bassoon and double bassoon. (Gunther Joppig Collection.)*
Photo: Koopmann.

Right: *Modern Buffet bassoon and contrebasson. (Works photo.)*

'Les musiciens de l'orchestre' by Edgar Degas (1834–1917). (Musée du Louvre, Paris.) The picture was painted in 1868 and shows members of the Paris Opera orchestra. Will Jansen has identified the flautist as Professor Henri Altés (1826–99) and the bassoonist as Désiré Dihau (1833–1909). Dihau was an uncle of Toulouse-Lautrec. He is playing a French Jancourt system bassoon.

Part of the Sinfonia,
Christmas Oratorio
Part II

Johann Sebastian Bach (1685–1750)

these instruments (or musicians who could play them) at his disposal in England. And Vivaldi, who wrote concertos for the most recondite instruments, does not seem to have made use of the oboe d'amore or similar instruments such as the oboe luongo, the oboe grande or the oboe basso (all in A). The sons of Bach, who were generally critical of their father's work, did not share his predilection for this instrument, which he often used to illustrate scenes of a pastoral character.

In the Classical period the instrument fell into oblivion, and in the middle of the nineteenth century, when people began to rediscover the works of Johann Sebastian Bach, there was no suitable instrument to play the oboe d'amore parts. If the solo passages could be played on the oboe they were transposed to C; if not, they were given to a cor anglais. This performance practice used to go unchallenged, for it was thought that the works of the past could only be performed in terms of the sonorities of one's own age. Wolfgang Amadeus Mozart's arrangement of Handel's *Messiah* and Richard Wagner's arrangement of Christoph Willibald Gluck's (1714–87) *Iphigenie in Aulis* are examples of this.

However, performers of Bach's music were soon no longer satisfied with this kind of interpretation and began to revive the instruments Bach had used. These attempts coincided with a general increase in historical awareness. Numerous societies and associations devoted themselves to publishing and collecting the forgotten works of old masters, and museums began to build up collections of musical instruments. The keeper of the Brussels collection, Victor-Charles Mahillon (1841–1924), was also the owner of a factory noted for its excellent instruments. In 1874 he began to make oboes d'amore, and the century of neglect was at an end. Mahillon naturally added to the oboe d'amore all the improvements that the modern oboe already possessed, so that nowadays we have a handful of original instruments from the Baroque era, and a few instruments from the end of the nineteenth century. Makers who specialize in oboes also tend to make the oboe d'amore, though there is a waiting list for new instruments on account of the small demand. Of all the members of the oboe family this is probably the one that occasions the player the greatest difficulty. Heinrich Christoph Koch's remark in the *Musikalisches Lexikon* (1802) is still valid today:

> The reason why this instrument . . . has fallen into disuse is probably none other than that absolutely clean intonation is even more difficult to achieve than in the case of the normal oboe.[55]

It is true that some firms of instrument makers have attempted to improve the intonation, yet the restricted repertoire means that musicians tend to play this instrument only at Easter and Christmas, and this is not long enough to become wholly familiar with its idiosyncracies. The circumstances surrounding performances of sacred music usually make playing in tune rather difficult anyway. The continual change from oboe to oboe d'amore and cor anglais is usually compounded by the low temperatures in badly-heated churches, which tend to make the strings go sharp and the wind go flat.

The delightful concerto and chamber music repertoire which provides opportunities to play the instrument in a secular context is far too little known. In 1971 the *Neue Bach-Ausgabe*, which is edited jointly by the Johann-Sebastian-Bach Institut in Göttingen and the Bach Archive in Leipzig, published a reconstruction of an A major concerto for oboe d'amore based on the harpsichord

The oboe and its lower relatives

1. *Normal oboe in C by Heckel, Biebrich, 1966.*

2. *Soprano sarrusophone in B flat by Couesnon, Paris, c 1910.*

3. *Oboe d'amore in A by Heckel, Biebrich, 1971.*

4. *Cor anglais in F by Heckel, Biebrich, 1966.*

5. *Heckelphone in C by Heckel, Biebrich, 1914.*

6. *Baritone sarrusophone in E flat by Gautrot-Marquet, Paris, c 1870.*

7. *Contrabass sarrusophone in E flat by Conn, Elkart, c 1920.*

(Gunther Joppig Collection.)
Photo: Frehn.

*Beginning of the oboe d'amore part (in A) of the Concerto in G
major for flute, oboe d'amore and basso continuo.*

*Another copy ascribed to Antonio Lotti (1667–1740) is in A
major.*

concerto BWV 1055 by Johann Sebastian Bach (1685–1750).[56]
Wilfried Fischer thinks that this concerto was written between
1717 and 1723 at a time when Bach was *Hochfürstlich Anhalt-
Cöthenischer Kapellmeister* to Prince Leopold of Anhalt-Köthen
(1694–1728). It is thus probably one of the earliest concertos for
oboe d'amore, together with an A major concerto for oboe
d'amore, strings and basso continuo that is usually ascribed to
Johann David Heinichen (1683–1729), though it may in fact
have been written by Antonio Lotti (1667–1740). Two sets of
parts were destroyed by fire in World War II, and only a later copy
of the score has survived.

Karl Ditters von Dittersdorf (1739–99) and Christoph
Graupner (1683–1760) also wrote concertos for the instrument,
and Georg Philipp Telemann (1681–1767) made frequent use of
it, two particularly good examples being the E major concerto for
flute, oboe d'amore, viola d'amore, strings and harpsichord, and
the concerto in G major for flute, oboe d'amore and basso
continuo, which also exists in an A major version ascribed to
Antonio Lotti.

The Cor Anglais

Whereas the oboe d'amore only occasionally makes an appearance in the symphony orchestra, the cor anglais is now a
permanent feature, even of small symphony orchestras. Larger
orchestras have a player who is solely responsible for the cor
anglais; in others this task is assigned to one of the second oboists.
On account of its name the cor anglais (or English horn) is often
mistaken for a brass instrument. Players of the basset-horn, a
member of the clarinet family, also tend to encounter this

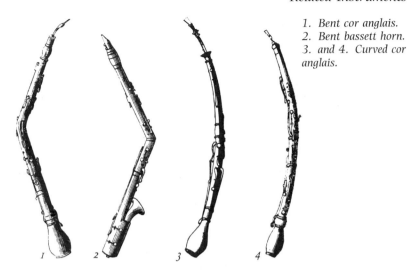

1. Bent cor anglais.
2. Bent bassett horn.
3. and 4. Curved cor anglais.

misunderstanding – though early basset-horns, with their markedly curved or bent form and their flared brass bell, to some extent deserved the epithet 'horn', particularly as the tone of the instrument in certain registers resembles that of a stopped horn. The literature on the subject is still divided with regard to the origin of the name 'English horn'. This term – cor anglais in English (American musicians nowadays prefer English horn) and *corno inglese* in Italian – first appeared at the beginning of the eighteenth century, and musicologists are at a loss when attempting to account for it. It would seem obvious to say that it means 'a horn from England'. Yet in view of its tone colour it is also conceivable that the epithet 'English' (in German this can also mean 'angelic') referred to the instrument's celestial sound; in other words, it was the 'horn of the angels'.

The modern cor anglais employs the same fingering as the oboe. Differences in the size of the holes, which used to render the change from oboe to cor anglais difficult, are nowadays overcome by means of the plateaux system and the corresponding location of the keys, so that the player, who is often required to change from the one to the other in the course of an orchestral work or a cantata, is no longer confronted with differing keywork. The range corresponds to that of the oboe, and the music is notated in such a way that, as we have seen, the player can use the same fingering as on the oboe. However, a written g' above middle c sounds a fifth lower. The cor anglais is a transposing instrument, and the composer has to take into account the difference between what is heard and what is notated, and has to write his cor anglais parts a fifth higher. Treating the cor anglais and other

March for oboe, taille and bass from the *Pfeifergericht 1752* in Frankfurt am Main.

related instruments as transposing instruments is of inestimable advantage to the player. On all these instruments he can apply to the written notes the fingering that he normally uses on his principal instrument, the oboe. This on the other hand causes problems for conductors and students of music who have to score-read at the piano and cope with transposing instruments in addition to the various clefs. Scores in which all the parts were written in C, in other words at their real pitches, did not get beyond some tentative attempts in the 1920s.

Other ways of writing the cor anglais part, such as the alto clef used in the old Bach complete edition (which reproduced the actual pitch) are fortunately not very common. In older scores one sometimes finds the cor anglais part written in the bass clef, a fourth below the real pitch. This kind of notation is also used for the basset-horn and the French horn.

There is still a lot of confusion about an instrument which is considered to be a predecessor of the cor anglais: the oboe da caccia. It appears in numerous works by Johann Sebastian Bach, including the St Matthew and St John passions, the Christmas Oratorio, and many cantatas, and is usually given obbligato passages. The 'hunting oboe' may derive its name from hunting horns which had a bent form and a flared bell, though it was also referred to as *Waldhautbois* ('forest oboe'). instruments by the Leipzig instrument maker Johann Heinrich Eichentopf (1678–1769) are considered to be true oboes da caccia; apart from a pronounced bent form they possess a brass bell,[57] which is also a feature of early basset-horns. Straight instruments in the alto register were called taille, tenor hautboy and vox humana. The oboe da caccia's flared bell was later discarded in favour of the pear-shaped 'love foot', though the bent form survived well beyond the middle of the nineteenth century in addition to an angled and perhaps even a straight form.

102

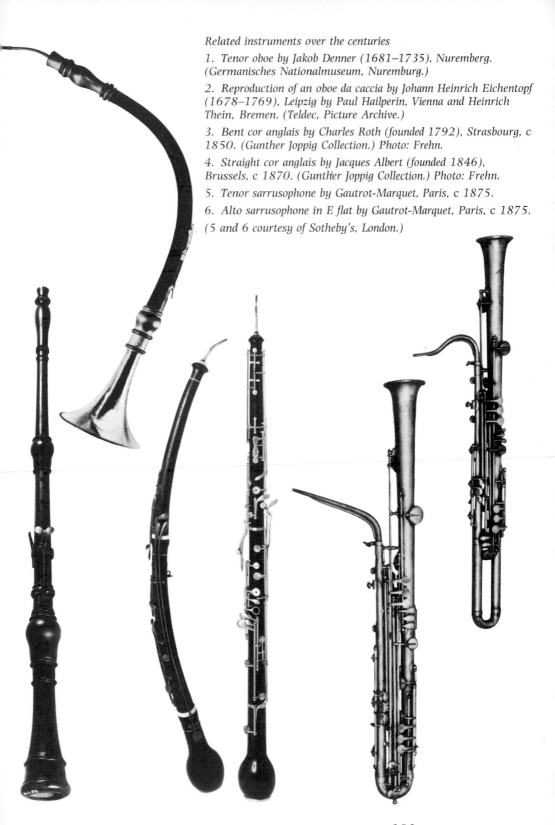

Related instruments over the centuries

1. Tenor oboe by Jakob Denner (1681–1735), Nuremberg. (Germanisches Nationalmuseum, Nuremburg.)

2. Reproduction of an oboe da caccia by Johann Heinrich Eichentopf (1678–1769), Leipzig by Paul Hailperin, Vienna and Heinrich Thein, Bremen. (Teldec, Picture Archive.)

3. Bent cor anglais by Charles Roth (founded 1792), Strasbourg, c 1850. (Gunther Joppig Collection.) Photo: Frehn.

4. Straight cor anglais by Jacques Albert (founded 1846), Brussels, c 1870. (Gunther Joppig Collection.) Photo: Frehn.

5. Tenor sarrusophone by Gautrot-Marquet, Paris, c 1875.

6. Alto sarrusophone in E flat by Gautrot-Marquet, Paris, c 1875.

(5 and 6 courtesy of Sotheby's, London.)

Trio für 2 Oboen und Alt-Oboe von L. v. Beethoven.*⁾

Komponirt im Jahre 1794.

Allegro.   Serie 8. N⁰ 63. Op. 87.

Excerpt from the first Complete Edition. Breitkopf & Härtel, Leipzig.

The oboe d'amore was no longer written for after the end of the Baroque era, though the predecessors of the modern cor anglais in its various guises and with its various names continued in use. As a middle register instrument it was equally at home in *Hautboistenbanden* and in chamber music groups. The genre of trios for two oboes and cor anglais was fairly common. Ludwig van Beethoven (1770–1827) wrote music for this combination after he had heard a 'new trio for two oboes and one cor anglais, as invented by Herr Wendt, performed by the brothers Johann, Franz and Philipp Teimer'[56] at a concert of the Vienna Tonkünstler-Sozietät on 23 December 1793. The Trio in C major for two oboes and cor anglais, Op. 87, was probably composed in 1794. It was followed in 1796 by the variations on *Là ci darem la mano* from Mozart's *Don Giovanni*, WoO28 (WoO = Works without opus numbers). The second of these pieces was not included in the first complete edition, for the publishers Breitkopf & Härtel rejected it on 20 September 1803. (More than a century was to elapse before they finally published it.)

A trio that Beethoven may well have heard was written by the oboist Johann Wenth (1745–1801). (It was published by

Adagio for cor anglais

Wolfgang Amadeus Mozart (1756–1791)

Ave verum corpus

Kneusslin in Basel in 1974 under the title *Divertimento in B flat*.) Wenth also made eight-part wind-band arrangements (for two oboes, two cor anglais, two French horns, and two bassoons) of Mozart's *Entführung aus dem Serail*, *The Marriage of Figaro* and *Così fan tutte*. This kind of arrangement was very popular. On 20 July 1782, after completing the opera *Così fan tutte*, Mozart wrote from Vienna to his father in Salzburg:

> Well, I am up to my eyes in work, for by Sunday week I have to arrange my opera for wind-instruments. If I don't, someone will anticipate me and secure the profits. And now you ask me to write a new symphony! How on earth can I do so? You have no idea how difficult it is to arrange something of this kind for wind-instruments, so that it suits the instruments and yet loses none of its effect. Well, I must just spend the night over it, for that is the only way; and to you, dearest father, I sacrifice it. You may rely on having something from me by every post. I shall work as fast as possible and, as far as haste permits, I shall turn out good work.[59]

Mozart left unfinished a quartet for cor anglais and three unspecified instruments. The entire solo part and about two thirds of the other parts of the Adagio movement K 580a were committed to paper, and there have been various attempts to

105

Andante pour le cor anglais.

complete the work. Its thematic material is related to the motet *Ave verum corpus* K618. Mozart also made use of the cor anglais in certain divertimenti and in the accompaniment of certain operatic arias. As much of the delightful chamber music for cor anglais composed towards the end of the Baroque era and in the Classical period is largely unknown – after all, the cor anglais is considered to be a typically Romantic instrument – I append a list of nine works which have been reissued in new editions. The names of the editors and publishers are given in brackets.

Johann Philipp Krieger (1648–1725): Partie 1704. (Seiffert. Kistner & Siegel)

Carl Biber (1681–1749): Sonata for two cor anglais, two violins and organ with cello, contrabass and bassoon ad lib. (Sherman. Universal Edition)

Joseph Haydn (1732–1809): Divertimento in F major for two violins, two cor anglais, two French horns and two bassoons. (Janetzky. Hofmeister)

Michael Haydn (1737–1806): Quartet in C for cor anglais, violin, cello and contrabass. (Rainer. Doblinger)

Johann Wenth (1745–1801): Quartetto concertante for oboe, oboe grande in B flat, cor anglais and bassoon. (Myslík. Kneusslin)

Johann Schenk (1753–1836): Quartetto for flute, two cor anglais and bassoon. (Steinbeck. Doblinger)

106

Cor anglais solo from Otello, *Act 1.*

Joseph Fiala (1754–1816): Three quintets for two cor anglais, two wood horns and bassoon. (Janetzky. Hofmeister)

Anton Reicha (1770–1836): Two Andantes and an Adagio for solo cor anglais, flute, clarinet, horn and bassoon. (Vester. Universal Edition)

Joseph Triebensee (1772–1846): Variations sur un thème de Haydn for oboes and cor anglais. (Myslík. Kneusslin)

There is also a handful of concertos for cor anglais and orchestra. Joseph Fiala composed one in E flat major, and Gaetano Donizetti (1797–1848) wrote an attractive concertino in 1816. The increased use of the cor anglais in the Romantic period for melancholy and elegiac scenes meant that the sound of the instrument acquired a one-sided connotation. A piece of mood-painting of this kind is a work by Bernhard Eduard Müller (1824–83), *Abendempfindung im Gebirge* (Evening mood in the

107

'Traurige Weise' *for cor anglais from* Tristan und Isolde.

Solo from Death and Transfiguration.

mountains) for solo cor anglais and orchestra. In Jean Sibelius's (1865–1957) *The Swan of Tuonela* the cor anglais symbolizes the song of the messenger of death. French composers avoid this kind of association by means of a more virtuoso treatment of the instrument. Examples are Arthur Honegger's (1892–1955) concerto da camera for flute, cor anglais and string orchestra, and Jean Françaix's (b. 1912) quartet for cor anglais and string trio (1971).

There are some memorable solo passages in operas by Giuseppe Verdi (1813–1901), Richard Wagner and Richard Strauss. Above are a few short excerpts.

The Baritone Oboe and Heckelphone

Certain oboe instruments that are pitched an octave below the oboe may be regarded as survivors of the old pommer family. Many of these instruments used to be called oboe da caccia, tenor hautboy, taille or tenor oboe, though today we tend to refer to all of them as baritone oboes in order to distinguish them from the real tenor instruments in F. The labelling of instruments on the basis of register does not always tally with their actual range; in families of instruments it tends to describe the relationship of the various members of the family, even if the range bears little relationship to the corresponding human voice. Some early baritone oboes are preserved in the Germanisches National-museum in Nuremberg.

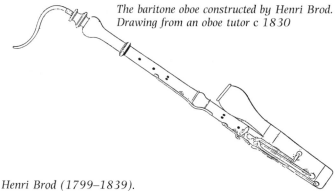

*The baritone oboe constructed by Henri Brod.
Drawing from an oboe tutor c 1830*

Henri Brod (1799–1839).

The basset oboe is an unusual instrument that seems to have been used only in those parts of Switzerland dominated by the Reformed Church (i.e. the Calvinists). For a long time this instrument, which has a rather wide bore, proved to be something of an enigma. Its origins, its music, and its use were largely unknown. The former director of the Beethoven House in Bonn, Professor Martin Staehelin, in an article published in the *Jahrbuch des Bernischen Museums*,[60] was the first to describe this musette bass or basset oboe in detail. His research revealed that *bassett oboe* or *musette bass* were not the original terms for this instrument, but rather names that first acquired common currency in the nineteenth century. It was used to accompany the singing of chorales (it should be remembered that the zealous reformers had initially banished all musical instruments from the church), and thus forms an interesting parallel to the oboe d'amore. Similarly, in the eighteenth and even in the nineteenth century, the singing of hymns in the Catholic church in France was accompanied by serpents, snake-like instruments which are considered to belong to the brass group. In the eighteenth century the oboe d'amore, as we have seen, was employed mainly in Protestant sacred music.

In the nineteenth century, particularly in France, there were attempts to enlarge the lower members of the oboe family. The length of the oboe bore was increased, with the result that the instruments did not differ markedly from the cor anglais, which we discussed above. The advantage was that, compared with the cor anglais the range increased a fourth at the bottom. Because of their great length many of these constructions had a bottom joint that doubled back on itself, thus resembling a bassoon butt joint.

Modern Heckelphone with Conservatoire – System from 1980 by William Heckel, Biebrich (Joppig Collection; photo Söffke, Hamburg).

A few examples of the baritone oboe, as it was known in France, have survived, yet by the end of the nineteenth century the instrument had not become widespread, and references to it in the literature are few and far between. In order to complete the confusion surrounding the name of this instrument, it should be added that it was often called bass oboe in England, merely in order to indicate that this was the lowest instrument of the oboe group. An especially beautiful example of a baritone oboe is now in the Berne museum.

Towards the end of the nineteenth century the firm of Lorée developed the first baritone oboe that could be taken seriously. It soon had a competitor produced by the famous bassoon maker, Wilhelm Heckel. Heckel, whose improved double bassoon had earned the approval of Richard Wagner, stated in his memoirs that the idea of the *heckelphone* in fact emanated from the latter. However, I have been unable to find corroborative evidence for this in the letters and diaries I have consulted. Heckel was a keen collector of musical instruments and was in touch with other collectors. Towards the end of the nineteenth century, while he was making reproductions of original instruments for them, he also produced a copy of a Swiss basset oboe. The heckelphone in fact has certain features in common with the basset oboe, in particular the very wide bore, and thus the idea that Wilhelm Heckel used the latter as the starting point for the design of his new instrument is not as far-fetched as it may seem. Of course the modern keywork meant that this was a completely new instrument. It was soon being played with great enthusiasm at various music festivals.

Richard Strauss and Max von Schillings (1868–1933) in particular made use of the instrument in their opulent scores, above all in their operatic works. In fact *Salome* (1905) and *Elektra* (1909) have kept the instrument alive. Richard Strauss's

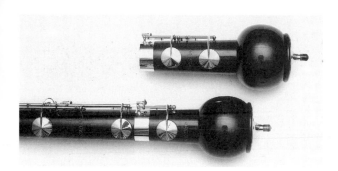

The two different bells of the Heckelphone (same date as opposite): for A (above) and B-flat (below).

ballet *Josephslegende*, which for many years was considered unperformable, has only recently been convincingly staged. It also contains a part for the heckelphone, as do two other works by him – the *Alpensinfonie* and the *Festliches Präludium*, an occasional work written in 1913 for the opening of the Konzerthaus in Vienna. The only problematical aspect of this truly excellent instrument is its name, for far too many instrument makers have sought to immortalize themselves by adding their names to the suffix 'phone'. Only a few have been successful. Yet to most listeners and musicians the significance of such names remains a closed book, and curious terms such as *heckelphone, sarrusophone, rothphone* and *saxorusophone* are meaningless. This 'labelling mania' unfortunately survives to this day. Only recently a musician has come up with an instrument with the recondite name of *pinschofphone*. The musician of course is called Pinschof; but it would be hard to guess that his invention is a bass flute with a head joint at right angles to the other joints.

On account of its voluminous sound the heckelphone is particularly suited, it seems, to the orchestral palette of the late romantic orchestra; at least it was almost exclusively employed by composers with a penchant for this style. The instrument appears neither in the works of the Second Viennese School, nor in those of composers born between 1910 and 1920. An exception to this rule is Edgar Varèse, who wrote for it in two of his works, *Arcana* and *Amériques*.

A trio by Paul Hindemith (1895–1963) for viola (which the composer himself played extremely well), heckelphone and piano is seldom played on account of the rarity of the heckelphone. It is one of Hindemith's best chamber music works. He was probably inspired to write it on one of his visits to the firm of Heckel, which are documented by entries in the visitors' book. (Hindemith also acquired a bassoon for his own small collection.)

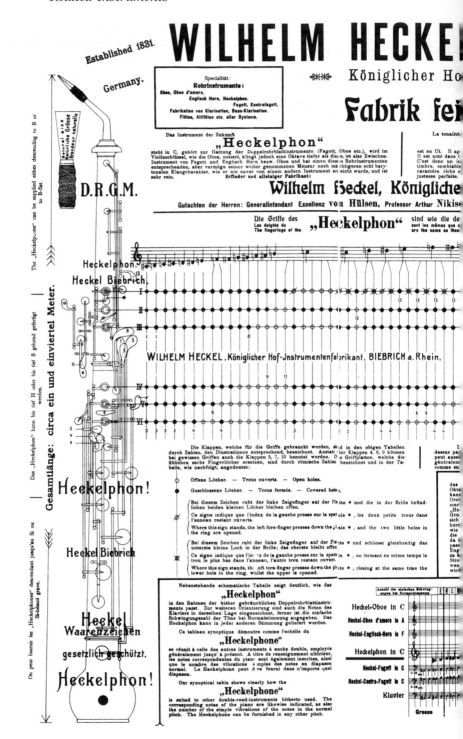

Fingering chart for the newly developed heckelphone (1904).

BIEBRICH A. RHEIN.

Instrumenten-Fabrikant.

Maison fondée en 1831.

Allemagne.

Sole agent for Great Britain & the colonies:
H. Lloyd, 10, Albany Road, Wolverhampton.

Seul représentant pour la France & les colonies:
S. Pélissier, 13, Rue des Deux-Ponts, Montpellier.

Sole agent for bassoons for the United States of North-America:
Carl Fischer, 6—10, Fourth-Ave., New-York.

las-Instrumente.

...lphone"

...truments à anche double, (Basson, hautbois etc.)
...ois, mais il sonne une octave au-dessous de celui-ci.
... le basson et le cor anglais ou le hautbois.
...ments à anche double, est très sonore et d'un
... été atteint auparavant; l'instrument est d'une
...seul fabricant:

The instrument of the future
„Heckelphone"

stands in C. It belongs to the family of the double-reed-instruments (Bassoon, oboe etc.) and is written in the treble-clef like the oboe, but sounds one octave below the latter. It is therefore an intermediate instrument between the bassoon and the cor anglais or oboe, and its tone, although resembling that of the said double-reed-instruments, is remarkable for its more powerful character such as has never before been attained; its tune is pure and perfect.
Inventor and sole manufacturer:

...rumenten-Fabrikant, Biebrich a. Rhein.

...r, Professor Schillings, Dr. Richard Strauss, Siegfried Wagner, Felix Weingartner u. a. siehe umseitig.

...chhorns. Das Instrument kann daher von jedem Oboer sofort geblasen werden.
...is. Tout hautboiste peut donc jouer cet instrument de suite sans aucun exercice.
... The instrument can therefore, immediately, be played by any oboe-player without having practised it.

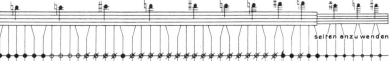

seiten anzuwenden.

GRIFFTABELLE.   **WILHELM HECKEL,** Königlicher Hof-Jnstrumentenfabrikant, BIEBRICH a. Rhein.

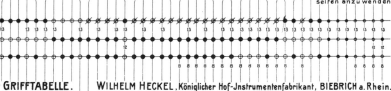

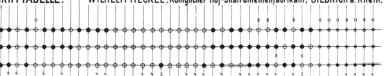

...s divers doigtés sont désignées dans la tablature ci-
...à ceux des illustrations. Au lieu des clefs 4, 6, 9 on
... les clefs 5, 7, 10. Les clefs remplaçant les six trous
... des chiffres romains et marquées dans la tablature

The keys, which are to be used for the various fingerings, are marked in the above table by numbers corresponding to the illustrations. Instead of the keys 4, 6, 9, one can take for certain fingerings the keys 5, 7, 10 respectively. The finger-plates, which are to supply the 6 finger-holes generally used, are marked by Roman numbers and indicated in the fingering-table as follows:

...aus der Tell-Ouverture von Rossini, welche, da
...immer auf dem Englisch-Horn und zwar eine
...sie vom Componisten ursprünglich gedacht ist,
...in richtiger Tonlage gespielt werden. In der
...lten im 1. Satz wie nebenstehend notiert; ich be-
...Cor ing. Stimme gleichzeitig die Stimme für das
...nstrument transponiert, eingeschaltet habe. Den
...rüngliche Absicht nicht durchführte, erklärt man
...Werk schrieb. schwebte ihm der Klang des Alpen-
...ge, in der das Heckelphon steht. Er notierte so,
...dachte an ein Tonwerkzeug in C und schrieb
...er nachher die Stimme herausschreiben wollte,
..., denn in dieser Tonlage gab es bis heute kein
...nsste der Meister notgedrungen die Stimme für
...ie dieselbe jetzt — wie gesagt, leider eine Oktave
...in der Orchester-Partitur steht nach wie vor die
...und dem Dirigenten thut es immer ins Ohr wehe,
...passende Stelle auf dem Englisch-Horn geblasen

Flauto
Clarinetti in La
Corni in Sol
Cor ing.
Heckelphon
Fagotti
Violini
Viola
Violoncelli
Contrabassi

Auf dem „Heckelphon" jedoch kann die Stimme in der Urtonlage geblasen werden mit einer dem Alpenhorn möglichst angenäherten Klangfarbe. Allerdings wird das Heckelphon im Violinschlüssel notiert, und zwar habe ich dies speziell aus dem Grunde so eingerichtet, weil ein Oboebläser diesen Schlüssel leichter liest, als den Bassschlüssel. Da nun das Heckelphon — siehe nebenstehende „Schematische Tabelle", die eine Ergänzung zu Wilhelm Heckel's be-

kannter, grossen schematischen Tabelle bildet — eine Oktave tiefer klingt, als es notiert wird, so würde die Stimme für Heckelphon so herauszuschreiben werden müssen, wie ich sie in obiger Partitur eingeschaltet habe, bleibt also so klingend, wie das Heckelphon im Bassschlüssel notiert wurde. Demnach ist also dieses grosse Problem gelöst und sollte diese Stelle in Zukunft nur von dem Instrument der Zukunft, dem „Heckelphon", geblasen werden.
Herr Dr. Richard Strauss sagt in seinem Gutachten über das Heckelphon, dass dasselbe sich vorzüglich zur traurigen Weise im Tristan eigne. — Gerade die für das Heckelphon verhältnismässig hohe Lage erzeugt bei dieser Melodie einen wehmütigen Klangcharakter. Die Tonlage bleibt hier dieselbe wie beim Englisch-Horn, nur muss, weil das Heckelphon in C steht, die Stelle transponiert werden, wird also so notiert:

Heckelphon
Mässig langsam
p cresc.   dim.   p

Heckelphon

...gestrichene   Zweigestrichene

Instrument verhältnismässig hohe Lage erzeugt bei dieser Melodie einen wehmütigen Klangcharakter. Die Tonlage bleibt hier dieselbe wie beim Englisch-Horn, nur muss, weil das Heckelphon in C steht, die Stelle transponiert werden, wird also so notiert:

Aber auch für die lustige Weise ist das Heckelphon wie geschaffen. Ausserdem ist der Vorteil damit verbunden, beide Soli auf einem Instrument blasen zu können. Nebenstehendes ist ein Bruchstück aus der lustigen Weise, für Heckelphon transponiert.
Es würde zu weit führen, hier alle die vielen Englisch-Horn-Solostellen aufzuführen, für welche das Heckelphon geeigneter erscheint, aber oben erwähnte Soli sind wohl zunächst als die wichtigsten zu bezeichnen.

Heckelphone bell in bass-clarinet shape by William Heckel, Biebrich 1909 (Musikinstrumentmuseum der Karl-Marx-Universität, Leipzig, no. 1353).

Unfortunately it soon became the rule to do without the heckelphone, even in Strauss operas. The parts were evenly divided between the bass clarinet and the first bassoon, and right up to the 1960s only the larger musical centres of Munich, Vienna and Hamburg possessed instruments and musicians able to play them. In the last few years the situation has changed somewhat. There is now an increased interest in adhering strictly to the score. As a result more instruments have been ordered, and these are now fitted with all the improvements common to modern oboes, oboes d'amore and cor anglais. However, many composers still consider it a risk to write for the heckelphone. The instrument remains largely unknown and only a handful of musicians own one and are prepared to play it. Compared to the oboe the embouchure requires some getting used to, particularly as players tend to use modified bassoon reeds in order to avoid having to buy reed-making equipment specially designed for the heckelphone (though these are in fact well suited to the task).

Hans-Werner Henze, Giuseppe Sinopoli, Hans-Joachim Hespos and Werner Schulze are among the younger composers who have looked favourably on the instrument and have written obbligato passages for it in their orchestral works. Continuing the late romantic tradition of the instrument, the Viennese composer Raimund Weissensteiner has composed a *Sonata for Heckelphone and Piano*. Recently the French have once again tried to revive the baritone oboe, and, since 1979 it has been made in France by Strasser-Marigaux, and also by Lorée and Rigautat. Those readers who are interested in the history and the repertoire of these fascinating baritone instruments are referred to the author's more comprehensive and detailed account, *Die Geschichte der Doppelrohrblattinstrumente von 1850 bis heute und ihre Verwendung in Orchester- und Kammermusik* (Verlag Das Musikinstrument. Frankfurt, 1980).[61]

Facsimile of the Arioso from the Op. 47 Trio by Paul Hindemith (1895–1963).

Heckelphone solo from snúningur, *five pieces for orchestra (1980) by Werner Schulze.*

The Sarrusophone

Originally designed to replace the oboe and the bassoon, which are not particularly suited to military purposes, the sarrusophones constitute a family of instruments that is largely unknown today. The idea of these instruments arose at a time when there was a great deal of interest in military music, and which witnessed lengthy studies of its character, of the various combinations of instruments, and of the national idiosyncracies. A good example of this is Georges Kastner's *Manuel Général de Musique Militaire*, which was published in 1848.

In the nineteenth century military bands gave large sections of the population a chance to hear music that could otherwise only be heard in opera houses and concert halls. The repertoire of these orchestras was not restricted to marches, but also included the latest popular hits, overtures, pot-pourris of well-known operas, and arrangements of famous symphonies and concertos. The military bands were the descendants of the *Feldmusik* (or corps of military musicians) which originally consisted of oboes and bassoons (or their predecessors, the pommers and dulcians), and which, as time went on, were augmented by French horns, trumpets and, later, clarinets. They were further augmented, especially in the bass and contrabass register, by the use of the serpent and, later, the ophicleide. Around 1850 the debate on which instruments should and could be included in military bands was in full swing.

The numerous military bands also provided work for many firms of instruments makers, and it is easy to understand why they attempted to ingratiate themselves with the bands by continually coming up with new inventions. A further factor was the lack of really effective low bass instruments, of which there was a dearth in bands that were continually increasing in size. Valves had not yet reached a stage where they were able to cope

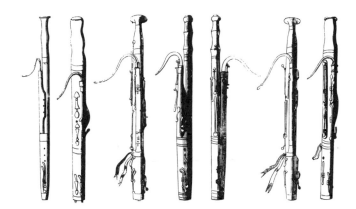

Military bassoon from Georges Kastner, Manuel Général de Musique Militaire *(Paris, 1848).*

with all the demands made on them, and thus musicians turned their attention to new constructions capable of surmounting these shortcomings. All this was spurred on by the popular competitions between military bands of different nations.

Adolphe Sax attempted to provide an answer to these problems by inventing and patenting whole new families of instruments such as the saxhorns and the saxophones. With the help of the French bandmaster Sarrus, Sax's competitor Pierre-Louis Gautrot (?–1882) developed a family of instruments which, though based on oboes and bassoons, were made of metal. Their wider conicity led to a great increase in sound in all registers. The prevalent belief in progress meant that these instruments were immediately fitted with the fingering system that Theobald Boehm had patented a few years earlier. However, there were important differences between this and previous fingering systems, and its seems that the difficulties likely to be encountered by those attempting to adapt to the new one were either not taken into account or simply ignored – once musicians have learnt to play an instrument they tend to be sceptical about innovations in general and fingering in particular, if they do not reject them out of hand. And so it was not easy to popularize saxophones and sarrusophones. In addition to this Gautrot ran into difficulties on account of a dispute with Adolphe Sax, who had patented the saxophone as early as 1846, whilst Gautrot first revealed his new instruments in 1856.

Whereas saxophones only slowly acquired a firm place in musical life, first becoming popular in the 1920s and 1930s on account of their role in jazz, the reverse was true of the sarrusophones. After initial successes in which the smaller members of the family gained some ground (at least this may be deduced from the instruments which have survived in collections), they gradually fell into disuse. It is a curious fact that the contrabass sarrusophone is found mainly in a sphere for which it was originally not intended, being used in numerous French scores in place of the double bassoon, which was bedevilled throughout the nineteenth century by a variety of shortcomings that can be traced back to the imperfections of the key mechanism.

The early double bassoons were, as we shall see below, rather unwieldy instruments and there were limits to what they could play. Over and above this their tone was uneven. Here the modern contrabass sarrusophone provided a real alternative, and thus the contrabass models were widely used. In the 1920s exact copies of the French Buffet-Crampon models were made in the United States, and fitted with all the latest technical improvements, such as raised tone holes – a technique that the American flute maker William S. Haynes invented and which he patented in America in 1914. Today the contrabass sarrusophone parts are unfortunately played by the double bassoon, which does not do justice to the composers' intentions.

A very late example of the use of this instrument is to be found in Igor Stravinsky's (1882–1971) 12-note work *Threni* (1957/58) for soloists, chorus and orchestra. The score of this work does not include bassoons, though a contrabass sarrusophone is used to emphasize the rhythmic accents, mostly together with the piano. The intended effect of a low F# played forte cannot be adequately rendered by a double bassoon in the same register. The same is true of the solo in Paul Dukas's (1865–1935) *The Sorcerer's Apprentice*, where, at the start of the second section, the motif first appears on the contrabass sarrusophone.

The higher members of the family are rarely used in serious music, though recently the West German composer Hans-

118

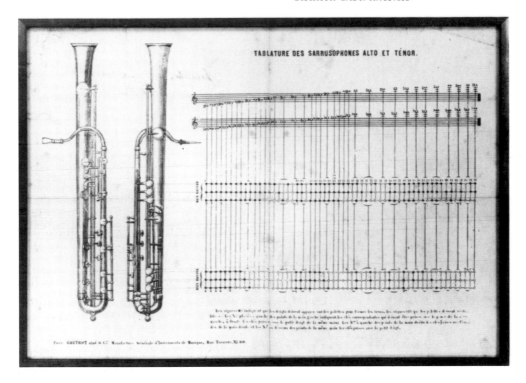

Fingering chart for alto and tenor sarrusophone. (Collection Buser, Binningen.)

Joachim Hespos has used the soprano sarrusophone in a composition entitled *Go* (1978). By combining it with other rare instruments (heckelphone, A flat clarinet, tárogató) Hespos achieved new and unusual colouristic effects. The sarrusophone comes in the following sizes: sopranino sarrusophone in E flat; soprano sarrusophone in B flat; alto sarrusophone in E flat; tenor sarrusophone in B flat; baritone sarrusophone in E flat; bass sarrusophone in B flat; contrabass sarrusophone in E flat; contrabass sarrusophone in C; contrabass sarrusophone in B flat. Those who wish to play the sarrusophone will have to adapt to the Boehm system, which is currently only used on flutes, and, in certain parts of the world, on clarinets. Attempts to use the Boehm system on the oboe (Boehm system oboes are depicted on page 82, no. 2 and page 87, no. 9) have never got very far. The so-called Sharpe oboe combines features of the Boehm and the

119

Excerpt from Threni.

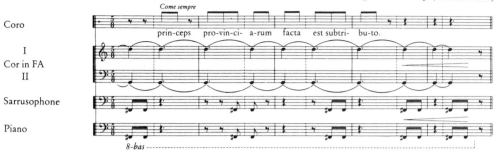

Igor Stravinsky (1882–1971)

Excerpt from The Sorcerer's Apprentice.

Paul Dukas (1865–1935)

French Conservatoire systems, yet these innovations have not become widely accepted. The high cost of a Boehm system bassoon usually discourages prospective buyers.

In the last few years there has been renewed interest in the sarrusophone, even though it virtually had to be reinvented, for many French instrument makers were no longer familiar with it. Perhaps the revival of medieval and Renaissance performance practice may one day lead to a renewed use of these instruments. Recordings of Beethoven symphonies played on original instruments have already appeared, and one of these days there will be a demand for playable sarrusophones. Quite a few contrabass sarrusophones have been made by the American firm of Conn, and in an early Sidney Bechet (1897–1959) recording one of the refrains is played on one of them. On page 99, no. 2, 6 and 7 we depict three sarrusophones (some of the crooks have been omitted for photographic reasons). The illustrations of the baritone and bass instruments show the ophicleide-like construction, which may be explained by the fact that Gautrot also made improvements to this instrument.

120

1. *Bass in B flat*
2. *Baritone in E flat*
3. *Tenor in B flat*
4. *Alto in E flat*
5. *Soprano in B flat*
6. *Soprano E flat*

The Rothphone and the Reed Contrabass

Among the many Italian instruments for military bands there is one that is still in use which combines a wide bore with the blowing mechanism of double reed instruments. It is called *Rohrkontrabass* (reed contrabass) in Germany and *Contrabasso ad ancia* in Italy. Its bore is wider than that of the contrabass sarrusophone, and it makes use of a system of fingering which corresponds to that of the ophicleide. In large Italian bands the reed contrabass continues to be used to this day, and the firm of Romeo Orsi in Milan makes a limited number of these instruments to order. Rothphones have in the past been ignored by organologists, even though a fair number of them must have been produced – at least that is what the instruments preserved in American collections suggest. Faced with the word rothphone it seems apposite to think of a combination of a maker's name with the suffix 'phone', and sure enough the *Index of Musical Wind-Instrument Makers* has the following entry under 'Roth':

Roth, Ferdinando [1815–98]:Milan. Founded 1832.
. . . Rothophone, alto in E flat, stamped < Brevetto Bottali > and < Flli. A.M. Bottali, Milano > H.C. Peterson:another in Boosey and Hawkes Coll'n. A Ricordi band-score of 1905 contains an advertisement of < Bottali (Antica marca Ferdo. Roth) > . It added < Rothfoni (Brevetto Bottali), Nuova Serie di instrumenti ad ancia doppia, a complemento del contrabasso ad ancia > . (Per A.C. Baines.) . . .[62]

121

The author playing the contrabass sarrusophone in a studio recording of Oskar Schlemmer's (1888–1943) Das Triadische Ballett. The music was written for the 1977 Berlin Festwochen by Hans-Joachim Hespos (b. 1938), who made use of a number of rare instruments to characterize the dancers. Photo: Trappe, Frankfurt am Main.

Related Instruments

Metal double reed instruments
1. Reed contrabass in form of a tuba made of brass, c 1870. (Horniman Museum, London.)

2. Metal double bassoon by Evette & Schaeffer, successors of Buffet-Crampon, c 1900.
(Gunther Joppig Collection.) Photo: Koopmann.

3. Reed bass with a keyboard-style system of closed keys by Rancilio, Milan, c 1900. (Horniman Museum, London.)

Gerard Hoffnung (1925–59): Collage with reed contrabass. (Verlag Langen-Müller. Munich/Vienna.)

Whereas the first two entries refer to rothphones preserved in collections, the advertisement in a wind-band score published by Ricordi roughly indicates the possible time at which the instruments were invented: before 1900. The author owns a quartet consisting of the soprano, alto, tenor and baritone instruments. The rothphones combine the construction of the saxophone with the embouchure of double reed instruments, though they are narrower than saxophones and sarrusophones, and have Boehm system fingering. The term *Saxorusophone*, which has also been used for this instrument, is actually more appropriate, for it immediately enables one to imagine an instrument that combines aspects of the saxophone and the sarrusophone. This family of instruments does not seem to have found widespread acceptance, even in Italy, and many experts have never heard of them. A rothphone quartet is depicted on p. 126.

The Double Bassoon

The double bassoon (or contrabassoon) is one of the most interesting double reed instruments. Its size alone is impressive. The story of its development is one of many setbacks, of persistent innovation, and of new constructions. In fact its present form is not particularly old, for it was only in 1879 that Wilhelm Heckel managed to design a double bassoon that was able to fulfil all orchestral requirements. Until that time the instrument still had a number of imperfections, and it is easy to understand why, although double bassoons have been made since the time of Handel, the instrument first acquired a permanent home in the orchestra in the twentieth century. The principal constructional difficulties associated with the double bassoon are the large dimensions of the tubes and the attendant long distances between the tone holes, which have to be bridged by means of keys. A modern double bassoon that can play low A has a tube length of 5.96 metres, and this can only be reduced to a manageable size by dividing it into four and by placing the tubes next to each other.

Early double bassoons were constructed on practically the same lines as normal bassoons and for this reason loomed up above the rest of the orchestra – a double bassoon of this kind from the time of Beethoven is depicted on page 28, nos, 1–5. On this instrument the hands are a fair distance apart and the tone holes, which are covered directly by the fingers, are so large that the player cannot afford the luxury of having short or podgy fingers. The lowest note on this instrument is contra C. Instruments called *Halbkontrafagott* (half double bassoons) only descended to low F or E flat.

These intermediate models were the reason why certain makers later referred to double bassoons descending to C', B flat'' or A'' as *subkontrafagott*. This in turn led people to believe that these were double bassoons which could play an octave lower than the normal double bassoon. Instruments of this kind, if they existed, would descend to C'', lower than the lowest note on the piano (which is occasionally heard on large church organs in combination with other stops).

A series of double bassoons was also developed by makers who were interested in the military band market. Their most important characteristic was the compact construction. In other words, it was essential that the instrument could still be played while the player was marching, and that it did not weigh too much. After the makers had overcome the problem of the keys and the key mechanism there was no end to the variations on this theme. As in the case of the ophicleides, these instruments had a key system in which all the keys were closed when playing the lowest note. To play the notes above, the keys were opened one

A quartet of rothphones consisting of

1. *Soprano rothphone in B flat by Prof. Romeo Orsi, Milan, c 1900.*
2. *Alto rothphone in E flat.*
3. *Tenor rothphone in B flat.*
4. *Baritone rothphone in E flat.*

2–4 by A.M. Bottali, Milan, c 1900.
(Gunther Joppig Collection. Photo: Koopmann.)

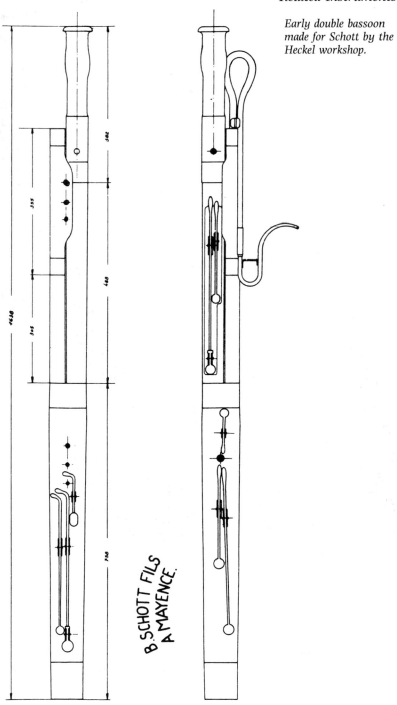

Early double bassoon made for Schott by the Heckel workshop.

B.SCHOTT FILS A MAYENCE.

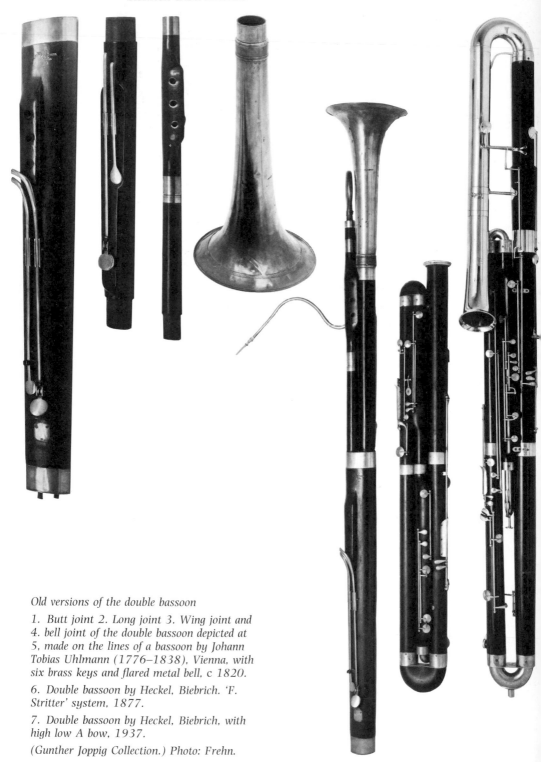

Old versions of the double bassoon

1. Butt joint 2. Long joint 3. Wing joint and 4. bell joint of the double bassoon depicted at 5, made on the lines of a bassoon by Johann Tobias Uhlmann (1776–1838), Vienna, with six brass keys and flared metal bell, c 1820.

6. Double bassoon by Heckel, Biebrich. 'F. Stritter' system, 1877.

7. Double bassoon by Heckel, Biebrich, with high low A bow, 1937.

(Gunther Joppig Collection.) Photo: Frehn.

Keyboard double bassoon by Carl Wilhelm Moritz (1811–55), Berlin. The Prussian patent was granted in 1856.

after the other. This kind of mechanism was sometimes combined with a piano-style keyboard, so that even wind players who were not familiar with the idiosyncracies of bassoon fingering were able to play this instrument provided they had mastered the embouchure. Instruments of this sort do not seem to have survived, but an illustration from a military periodical, *Soldatenfreund*, shows a military musician with a double bassoon of this kind.

The smallest double bassoon was the work of that brilliant maker and improver of bassoons, Wilhelm Heckel. Together with his head craftsman Friedrich Stritter (1850–1922), he developed an instrument which made good use of even the smallest corners, so that the size and especially the weight were greatly reduced. The patent made a point of emphasizing that the instrument was suited to marching.

Yet it is not quite clear why it was supposed to have been more manageable on account of its fingering system, which was diametrically opposed to that of the normal bassoon. The bent tubes and the small size of the instrument meant the high notes between c and f, which are normally played by the left hand, ended up at the bottom of the instrument, and the low notes for the right hand at the top end, so that it had to be held to the left and not to the right. When one plays this instrument it is disconcerting to find the higher notes lower down the instrument

– something which occurs on no other wind instrument. Perhaps that was the reason why this model was never very popular. In addition to the signature 'Wilhelm Heckel' surviving instruments are usually stamped 'System Stritter', and often have a regimental mark – proof that they were used in military bands.

The instrument depicted on page 128, no. 6 between the Uhlmann double bassoon (*c* 1820) and the tall version of the modern double bassoon (1937) looks rather small and graceful, although it can reach the same low notes as the Uhlmann double bassoon. The tall version is still being made in East Germany, whereas most of the firms that make double bassoons (Heckel, Fox, Amati, Kreul & Moosmann, Schreiber, Mollenhauer and Püchner) nowadays prefer the kind of instrument on which the low A metal bell is bent downwards to the vicinity of the right hand. This type of instrument gives the player a better view of the conductor, though the sound does not project as well. (*See colour page xiii.*) The French *contrabasson* is also a tall instrument that corresponds more to the kind that used to be made in Germany.

In addition to strengthening the bass line – double basses in particular are often not loud enough at the bottom end of the register – the double bassoon has been and is used for solo passages. There is an important example of this in the last movement of Beethoven's Ninth Symphony, where the composer achieves a special effect with the help of the low notes; it is as if a wind band were approaching from afar. Only the low instruments are heard at the beginning, to be gradually joined by the middle voices, until at last the top voices become audible. This effect is based on what actually happens when a military or wind band approaches the listener. Perhaps Beethoven wished in this way to symbolize the idea of joy permeating the whole world. Although orchestras in the romantic era continued to increase in size, the double bassoon was seldom used on account of its

FR. STRITTER ᴉɴ BIEBRICH.

Ganz aus Holz construirtes Contra-Fagott.

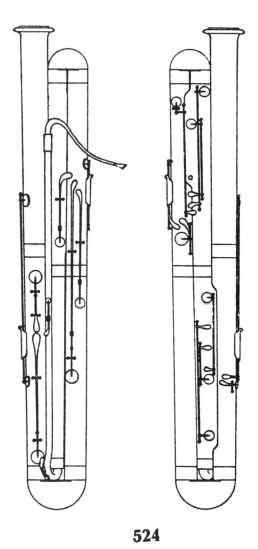

524

PHOTOGR. DRUCK DER KÖNIGL. PREUSS. STAATSDRUCKEREI.

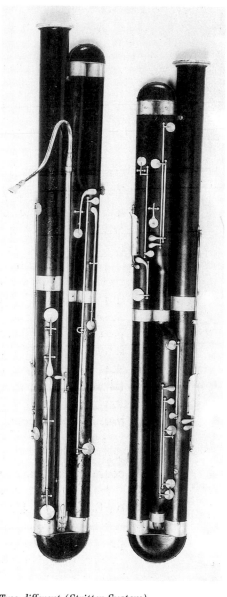

Two different (Stritter System) contrabassoons by Heckel, end of 19th century. Left: back of low-pitch model; right: front of high-pitch model.

Drawing from the patent of 1877.

Part of the fourth movement of the Ninth Symphony.

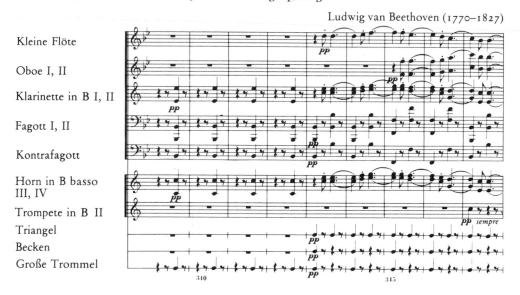

Ludwig van Beethoven (1770–1827)

imperfections. In *Salome* Richard Strauss stipulated that the famous double bassoon passage was only to be played by a double bassoon if there was a very good player. Otherwise it was to be played an octave lower, where possible, on the bassoon.

All low instruments have in common the ability to play very high notes (in relation to their range), and thus composers occasionally write very high passages for the double bassoon. In modern orchestras the instrument is usually played by the second or third bassoonist, who has to change from one to the other in certain pieces, e.g. Mahler symphonies requiring three bassoons and a double bassoon, where the third bassoonist has to change to the double bassoon. However, in very large orchestras there is an extra bassoonist for these passages, so the need to change in the course of a concert, which is always a problem, is obviated.

For some time the double bassoon has also been seen as a solo instrument in its own right, and not merely as an extension of the bassoon, and as a result there are now some solo pieces for it. Yet only a handful of musicians have concentrated exclusively on the instrument. One of them is the Viennese player Werner Schulze, who often assigns solo passages to the double bassoon in the Austrian Wind Quintet, of which he is the director. Recently he

132

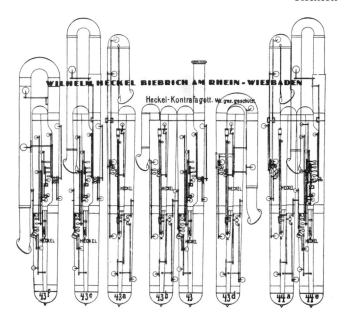

Different versions of the Heckel double bassoon.

Part of the Parsifal *'Vorspiel'.*

has made use of the contrabass sarrusophone and the heckelphone in some of his compositions. Although Richard Wagner made such complimentary remarks about Wilhelm Heckel's new double bassoon in 1879, he only used the instrument in his last opera, *Parsifal*, a short excerpt from which is quoted here.

SEVEN

The Role of the Oboe and the Bassoon in the Orchestra

In the eighteenth century the transition from the Baroque to the pre-Classical period witnessed the rise of a unique kind of orchestra that was to form the basis of the Classical and subsequently of the Romantic style. The uniform string section now consisted of first and second violins, violas, cellos and double basses (which often did not have a line of their own, but doubled the cellos at the lower octave). Sacred music, e.g. that of early Mozart, Michael Haydn and Joseph Haydn, often did not include a viola. But from the very beginning these orchestras included a pair of horns, which were complemented by a pair of oboes.

The concept of the *harmonieinstrument* probably originated at this time, for in pre-Classical symphonies the two oboes and two horns frequently have to play held chords. In addition to this they are given short solo passages that imitate the strings. Recent research into the operas of Joseph Haydn has shown that oboists also played the transverse flute and, on occasion, the bassoon. Certain Haydn operas written at Eszterháza include a pair of oboes and a pair of flutes, but the instruments never appear together: the scoring merely changed as the opera progressed. As the lists of payments made to the musicians do not mention flautists, we may assume that the oboists also played the flute, changing from one instrument to the other as and when required.[63]

Although many scores do not expressly stipulate bassoons, it may be assumed that they were in fact used to strengthen and support the lower strings – a familiar continuo practice that had been used in the Baroque era. The manner in which the oboe was employed in the orchestra supports the belief that it was held in high esteem. Composers would hardly have assigned so many solo passages to the oboe if it had been a crude, shrill-sounding instrument, possibly even played by an incompetent musician with little or no training. That string passages often alternate

Part of Symphony in A major K 201

Wolfgang Amadeus Mozart (1756–1791)

Excerpt from Symphony in A major K 201.

Wolfgang Amadeus Mozart (1756–1791)

with solo passages for the first oboe shows that the musicians were well able to play in tune in the high register on instruments that at this time only possessed the two c' and d sharp' keys; and whenever the oboe repeats what the strings have just played the listener can compare the tonal quality, the intonation and the skill of the musicians concerned.

Quite occasionally oboists exchanged their oboes for the cor anglais in order to introduce a different tone colour into the orchestra. Yet this happened less often in orchestral works than in the harmoniemusik of *Regimentshautboisten* and the small wind ensembles of the princely courts. (*See the section on the cor anglais.*) A good example of the orchestral use of the instrument is Joseph Haydn's Symphony No. 22, which has acquired the

Excerpt from Symphony No. 22, The Philosopher

Joseph Haydn (1732–1809)

nickname *The Philosopher*. In the symphonies and concertos of the Viennese classical period flutes appeared in pairs, as did bassoons. The clarinet, which now became a regular member of the orchestra, did not supplant the oboe. In fact its original function was to replace the trumpet, whose complicated playing technique had fallen into disuse on account of the dissolution of the trumpeters' guilds. Thus the earliest clarinet concertos are, with regard to the motivic character of the solo part, more like contemporary trumpet concertos than oboe concertos.

The wind section of the classical symphony provided the composer with a wide range of possible combinations.[64] For example, the oboes frequently doubled the bassoons. Those instances where part of the oboe melody is taken up and continued by the clarinet, the flute and the bassoon are particularly colourful. This kind of writing was evidently so pleasing both to listeners and composers that a special genre arose, the concertante symphony, in which wind instruments or a combination of wind and string instruments formed a solo group set off against the orchestra.

The demands made on the solo instruments are a sign of a high standard of musicianship. In concertante symphonies woodwind instruments have to play music of an unusual degree of difficulty. This genre also influenced the treatment of wind instruments in the orchestra in general. Soon even the run-of-the-mill orchestral oboist, whether he had ambitions as a soloist or not, had to play passages which even today, on our high-tech instruments, are as difficult as ever.

Mozart's Symphonie Concertante for flute, oboe, horn, bassoon and orchestra, which was written in Paris in 1778, is no longer extant, though we know of its existence from the composer's letters:

*Joseph Haydn (1732–1809). Engraving
by Francesco Bartolozzi, 1791.*

I am now going to compose a sinfonia concertante for flute,
Wendling; oboe, Ramm; horn, Punto; and bassoon, Ritter.[65]

The scoring of the Symphonie Concertante for oboe, clarinet,
bassoon and orchestra is different yet again. The authenticity of
this work has been called into question, yet it is an interesting
piece that presents the soloists with a number of challenges. In
1792 Joseph Haydn wrote a Symphonie Concertante for the
London concerts of Johann Peter Salomon (1745–1815). It was
first performed by Salomon (violin), Menel (cello), Harrington
(oboe), and Holmes (bassoon), and received enthusiastic reviews.
In view of successes of this kind, with outstanding soloists, it is
not surprising that in their symphonies and operas Haydn,
Mozart and Beethoven assigned exposed solo passages to the oboe
and the bassoon. They are some of the most important things an
oboist or a bassoonist has to learn as a student; and in the band-
room or on the concert platform one keeps on hearing oboists
practising the runs from the overture to Mozart's *Così fan tutte* or
bassoonists practising the tricky staccato passage from the fourth
movement of Beethoven's Fourth Symphony.

In his youth Beethoven came across some outstanding players
who were in the service of the Electoral court in Bonn, and he
probably wrote some pieces for them. It is thought that the Three
Duos for clarinet and bassoon, WoO 27, were composed around
this time. The art of instrumentation evolved by Mozart and
Beethoven was destined to influence not only the German-

137

speaking parts of Europe, but also other countries such as France. Hector Berlioz (1803–69) took 22 of the 66 full score examples in his treatise on orchestration[66] from the works of Mozart (five) and Beethoven (17); and the index of François-Auguste Gevaert's (1828–1908) *Traité Général d'Instrumentation* (1863) mentions Beethoven 28 times, Giacomo Meyerbeer (1791–1864) 25 times, and Mozart 20 times. Richard Wagner also referred to Beethoven when discussing the treatment of orchestral instruments, and his essay 'Über das Dirigieren' (1869) contains the following comment:

> The best hints I ever had for the tempo and phrasing of Beethoven's music were those I once derived from the soulful, sure-accented singing of the great Schröder-Devrient; it since has been impossible for me to allow e.g. the affecting cadenza for the oboe in the first movement of the C minor symphony

> to be draggled in the way I have always heard elsewhere. Nay, harking back from this cadenza itself, I also found the meaning and expression for that prolonged fermata of the first violins in the same passage, and the stirring impression I won from this

> pair of insignificant-looking points gave me a new insight into the life of the whole movement.[67]

Bassoon solo from the Sinfonia concertante.

Wolfgang Amadeus Mozart (1756–1791)

Beginning of the cadenza in the Sinfonia concertante

Joseph Haydn (1732–1809)

Beginning of Duo No. 1.

Ludwig van Beethoven (1770–1827)

The works of Richard Wagner, Franz Liszt (1811–86), Johannes Brahms (1833–97), Anton Bruckner (1824–96), Richard Strauss (1864–1949) and Gustav Mahler (1860–1911) also contain important and sometimes rather taxing parts for both the oboe and the bassoon.

EIGHT

Solo Literature for Oboe and Bassoon

In this section we will try to give some account of the skill and musicianship of oboists and bassoonists as mirrored in the concerto literature of the various epochs by referring to contemporary accounts and letters. In the context of this book we will of course have to restrict ourselves to a brief survey of the most significant works. Yet the most important evidence for the evaluation of the art of earlier generations of musicians is no doubt the concerto repertoire, which of course also reflects the taste of the times. Concertos were always written in collaboration with a particular artist or were commissioned by him, and the composer always did his best to make full use of the soloist's expertise in order to give him plenty of opportunity to show what he could do.

For a long time the debate concerning the musical capabilities of old instruments centred on the question of whether or not it is in fact possible to use them in the concertos in the form that they have been handed down to us, and on whether they could actually be played properly. It was claimed that these concertos were not only played much more slowly than indicated by the composer, but that the intonation must have been excruciatingly bad. Ideas of this kind rested on occasional attempts to play old instruments with reeds from modern instruments which were often not suited to them. The standards of modern musicians are often taken as a touchstone, and it is all too easy to forget the fact that sophisticated performing traditions may have been lost forever.

The revival of Baroque and Classical music – and especially the rediscovery of minor masters – has led to the emergence of a completely different picture. Numerous concertos by long forgotten composers have reappeared, and with the music other source material that has forced us to revise our opinions concerning earlier generations of musicians. The quotation from Leopold

Mozart in particular shows that musicians at the end of the eighteenth and the beginning of the nineteenth century were conscious of the necessity of playing in tune. This is proved by enthusiastic as well as disparaging remarks about the style of solo oboists and bassoonists. In our century the patient research work of a few dedicated musicians has enabled us to perform many concertos in the style of the time in which they were composed. The nineteenth century tends to be thought of as the age of the virtuoso, yet the demands made on the musician did not increase equally in the case of the various instruments, for the piano, the violin and the relatively new clarinet were favoured at the expense of the other woodwind and brass instruments. The few oboe concertos that were composed at this time, some of them of high quality, show clearly that the standard of playing was lower than in the case of Baroque and Classical concertos.

A number of factors were responsible for this development. For one thing a tradition of playing based on instruments with few keys had died out, and for another the musical style had changed inasmuch as all instruments were now required to play in all keys, which could only be reasonably achieved by making use of even more keys. For this reason a new kind of instrument had to be invented which could overcome all the drawbacks associated with the use of further keys, and a new generation of musicians able to produce the best possible results with these instruments was needed. In the case of woodwind instruments this process continued throughout the nineteenth century.

The clarinet had a rather more favourable start in all this. As a relatively young instrument that had been greeted with great enthusiasm, just as the oboe had been a century earlier, it already possessed certain improvements that had originally been made on other instruments. At the beginning of the nineteenth century the clarinet already possessed the most keys of any wind instrument and its tuning had been perfected. On account of its tonal properties it corresponded more nearly to the expressive requirements of the Romantics than the oboe. In fact the oboe and the bassoon in their present form have only been in existence for about a hundred years – not a long time for the establishment of generally accepted playing traditions.

Today there are once again oboe and bassoon soloists who can be compared to those of the past. Some of them are briefly described in the chapter entitled 'Famous oboists – then and now' (page 156). But whereas future generations will be able to judge the virtuosity of present-day soloists on the basis of records and radio recordings, we now have only the concertos (and of course the descriptions of their playing) on which the fame of the virtuosos of the past was founded.

Of the concertos by Alessandro (II) Besozzi, who has already been mentioned (*see p. 57ff.*) only a concerto in G major has been published. Others have been preserved as manuscripts in various libraries. The concerto is rather baroque in character. Even on modern instruments the figurations, broken chords and runs are not always easy to perform, in particular the passage in the third movement (Allegro) with its broken C major, B major and F# major triads, sevenths and ninths. We have already had cause to mention Johann Christian Fischer (p. 60ff.) The Minuet from his first oboe concerto appeared in numerous arrangements, and many contemporary musicians were obviously familiar with it. In the Kunstindustrie Museum in Oslo there is a picture which shows a French officer playing the work on a harp.

The slow movement of Johann Christian Bach's B flat Symphony has a big oboe solo that was written for Fischer (who was a close friend of his). Concerto No. 2 does not reach the level of the great concertos of Haydn and Mozart with regard to the thematic material and its elaboration, yet it contains interesting

142

Detail of a painting showing a music book opened to show Johann Christian Fischer's Minuet, c 1770. (Kunstindustrie Museum, Oslo.)

passages which give us an inkling of how Fischer played the two-key instrument. The portrait of the great oboist (*see colour page xiv*) shows him standing in front of an upright desk immersed in the study of a piece of music; on the table is his oboe, the C' and D sharp' keys of which are clearly visible. The instrument does not seem to have had any other keys. Bars 91 to 93 were probably not easy to play on this instrument.

Several concertos by Ludwig August Lebrun (1752–90) have also survived, some of them for oboe. Concerto No. 4 in C major was published in 1777. Its key, treatment of the instrument and melodic material are reminiscent of the Haydn concerto, and it also avoids the highest notes in the third octave above middle C. It is a surprising fact that the sources of all the great oboe concertos,

Thomas Gainsborough (1776).
Johann Christian Bach (1735–82).

Oboe solo

insofar as they have survived, are extremely patchy. In the case of the C major concerto for oboe and orchestra by Joseph Haydn there is some doubt about the work's authenticity. The Haydn expert, H.C. Robbins Landon, is of the opinion that it is not a genuine work; and in fact there are awkward passages in the part-writing, superfluous repetitions and longueurs which in the

Part of the second movement of the Symphony in B flat major.

Johann Christian Bach (1735–1782)

opinion of many a musicologist would not have been committed by Haydn. (There are two manuscripts, in Vienna and in Dresden, but both of them are copies.) If the concerto is by Haydn, then it is surely an early work. Yet there are also certain features which seem to point to Haydn's authorship; for example, the character of the thematic material in the third movement, which

144

Theme of the third movement from the oboe concerto.

«Es klappert die Mühle . . .»

is reminiscent of the folksong 'Es klappert die Mühle am rauschenden Bach'.

The source situation is equally unclear in the case of Mozart's Concerto for oboe and Orchestra K 314, which oboists are forced to share with flautists on account of an extant copy in D major. Recently a fragment of this concerto in Mozart's handwriting has been rediscovered, which makes it quite clear that the original key was C major; yet not enough of it has survived to enable us to

state unequivocally that the later flute concerto is merely an exact transposition. It is also unclear how many oboe concertos

Mozart actually wrote. In some of his letters he asks for the oboe concerto 'for Ferlendis'. Elsewhere he mentions that Ramm (*see pp. 62, 137 and 159*) had played Ferlendis's concerto on a number of occasions. Giuseppe Ferlendis (1755–1802) was a famous oboe and cor anglais virtuoso who became a member of the Salzburg Court Orchestra in 1777, and met the Mozart family on a number of occasions. But on 31 July 1778 Leopold Mozart wrote to the Prince-Bishop, Ignaz Joseph von Spaur, 'The oboist Ferlendis gave notice yesterday without warning in order to go to Vienna, and now we're left without a principal oboe'.

Ludwig van Beethoven
(1770–1827).
Engraving by Johann Neidl, 1800.

Johann Nepomuk Hummel
(1778–1837).
Engraving by Franz
Wenk.

Oboists like the two concertos – whether or not they are by Haydn or do or do not represent the original version – and have to be able to play them faultlessly when auditioning for a job in an orchestra. In passing it is worth mentioning that clarinettists have similar problems when it comes to the original version of Mozart's Clarinet Concerto, though this poses even greater problems for musicologists. A concerto for oboe and orchestra in E flat, known in the past as K Anhang H 294b, used to be ascribed to Mozart. In 1970 it was republished in a revised version without any information regarding its origins.

A concerto for oboe by Ludwig van Beethoven has unfortunately not been found, despite the efforts of many musicologists who have attempted to locate it. That this concerto once existed is deduced from a list of incipits (i.e. the beginnings of movements) that an unidentified nineteenth century copyist made on a sheet of music paper. It was common practice for concertos to be passed from hand to hand and for each musician to make a copy if he required one, and so one hopes that one of these days the work will turn up – unfortunately only a fraction of the manuscript holdings in public and private collections has been catalogued and evaluated.

The increasing interest in woodwind instruments suggests that many a long-lost treasure will one day reappear. For example, only a few years ago a work for oboe and orchestra by Johann Nepomuk Hummel (1778–1837), the Adagio and

Tema Allegretto

Variations Op. 102, came to light. Hummel was a contemporary of Beethoven, and, like him, one of the best pianists of his age. In

147

this piece one can study the oboe's expressive range from cantabile melody to fast staccato. The introductory Adagio with its wide melodic arches has a rather mournful character, whereas the following Allegretto theme with its folksong-like melody and its dance rhythms is full of life. In the two ensuing variations the use of diminishing note values (quavers, quaver triplets) gives the impression of increasing speed, though the tempo remains the same. Whereas the third variation is rather pensive in mood, the fourth, with its rapid runs, makes great demands on the player. This variation then merges into a development section (desinvolvimento) in which the theme of the introductory Adagio is combined with the theme of the variations. Thereupon the variation theme reappears to reveal its dance character in the form of a 3/4 waltz theme. Two alternativo sections follow and form the conclusion of the piece.

Little known and therefore infrequently played are the concertos of Frantisek Krommer, who was baptized as Frantisek Vincenc Kramár (1759–1831), and is therefore known as Kramár-Krommer. The Op. 37 concerto and the Op. 52 concerto are both in F major, and full of difficult passages which make high demands on the oboist. Certain passages in the third movement of the Op. 52 remind one of Mozart's quartet for oboe and string trio K 370. Like Mozart, Karmár-Krommer makes full use of all of the oboe's capabilities. The demands on embouchure are great because low passages are immediately followed by others which lead to the top notes, right up to f″′. Kramár-Krommer also added to the genre of trios for two oboes and cor anglais; his trio in F major includes variations on a theme by Pleyel, and was first published in 1979.

Vincenzo Bellini (1801–35) became famous on account of his operas *Norma* and *La Sonnambula* – with Rossini and Donizetti he was one of the great masters of bel canto. His concertino for oboe

148

Part of the third movement of the oboe quartet, K 370.

Wolfgang Amadeus Mozart (1756–1791)

Part of the third movement of the Op. 52 oboe concerto.

František Kramár-Krommer (1759–1831)

Beginning of the F major Variations on a theme by Pleyel.

František Kramár-Krommer (1759–1831)

and orchestra is an early work, yet it already places great emphasis on the oboe's singing quality. A *Larghetto cantabile* is followed by a captivating *Allegro polonese* in 3/4. This movement has the form of a rondo with the pattern ABACAB followed by a short coda.

A virtuoso passage from the Op. 110 oboe concerto.

Johann Wenzeslaus Kalliwoda (1801–1866)

A technically demanding passage from Sonata II (published in 1645).

Giovanni Antonio Bertoli

The violinist Johann Wenzeslaus Kalliwoda (1801–66) also wrote a virtuoso Concertino for Oboe and Orchestra Op. 110 that makes exhaustive use of the instrument's possibilities and at one point reaches g′′′. This note hardly ever occurs in the fingering charts of contemporary German oboe tutors, though the French included it in their studies. In the concerto literature of the time it is the exception rather than the rule. This concerto is of interest inasmuch as it represents an attempt to transfer to the oboe the improvements, particularly as regards technique, that had been

150

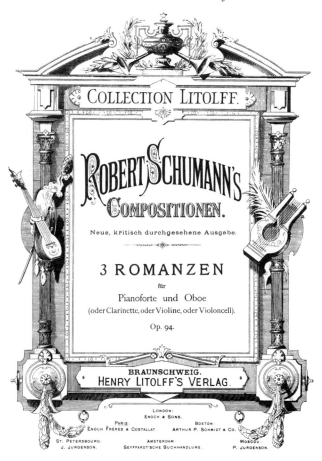

COLLECTION LITOLFF.

ROBERT SCHUMANN'S COMPOSITIONEN.

Neue, kritisch durchgesehene Ausgabe.

3 ROMANZEN

für

Pianoforte und Oboe

(oder Clarinette, oder Violine, oder Violoncell).

Op. 94.

BRAUNSCHWEIG.
HENRY LITOLFF'S VERLAG.

LONDON:
ENOCH & SONS.

PARIS: BOSTON:
ENOCH FRÈRES & COSTALLAT   ARTHUR P. SCHMIDT & CO.

ST. PETERSBOURG: AMSTERDAM: MOSCOU:
J. JURGENSON.   SEYFFARDT'SCHE BUCHHANDLUNG.   P. JURGENSON.

achieved on the piano and the violin. For this reason cantabile passages are of secondary importance. Unfortunately only a few works for the oboe were composed in the Romantic period. Exceptions are the Three Romances, Op. 94, by Robert Schumann (1810–56), which also appeared in versions for clarinet, violin or violoncello. Johannes Brahms assigned an important role to the oboe in his orchestral works, but he neglected the instrument in his chamber music works in favour of the clarinet.

In the Romantic era a genre arose that misused the oboe for fairly dubious effects. An example of this is the nocturno (*sic*!) *Alpenreigen and rondoletto pastorale* for oboe and piano Op. 17 by Rudolf Tillmetz, which overdoes the association of the sound of shawms and the rural mood. On about the same level are compositions by Friedemann with the title 'Marital chatter for oboe, bassoon and orchestra' or a work by a certain Mückenberger entitled *The Shepherd and the Shepherdess*, which is also a fantasy for oboe, bassoon and orchestra.

A heartening exception to these pieces, which, as nineteenth century concert programmes demonstrate, were in fact rather popular, is the Concertstück für Oboe and Orchester, Op. 18, by August Klughardt (1847–1902), which combines the sound of the oboe with that of the Romantic orchestra. Also little-known are the variations on a theme by Mikhail Glinka for oboe and military band by Nikolai Rimsky-Korsakov (1844–1908), which he composed in his capacity as inspector of Russian military music.

One of the most important concertos of the twentieth century is the Concerto for oboe and orchestra by Richard Strauss (1864–1949), which was written at the request of an American officer in 1946. In this work Strauss reverts to old virtuoso traditions; the long cantilena lines make great demands on the soloist.

The oldest bassoon sonatas by Giovanni Antonio Bertoli have already been mentioned. They were probably written for a dulcian with a range of exactly two octaves from C to c′ – the third and fourth octaves are not used. Nevertheless, the bassoonist for whom these pieces were written must have been very good, for the three sonatas, which were published as early as 1645, are full of runs, broken chords and leaps which even a player with a modern instrument could not play at sight. A few years later Joseph Bodin de Boismortier (1691–1765) was also writing rather difficult parts for the bassoon; in his Op. 26 Bassoon

Concerto he did not hesitate to write rather high notes. The work shows how much progress bassoonists had made within the space of a few years. In some of his chamber music works Boismortier also included interesting passages for the bassoon.

Excerpt from the solo part of the Op. 26 bassoon concerto.

Joseph Bodin de Boismortier (1691–1765)

We have already mentioned Johann Christian Bach, the youngest son of Johann Sebastian Bach, in connection with Johann Christian Fischer. J.C. Bach wrote a bassoon concerto in B flat that must have presented the musicians of the time with considerable difficulties. It is noticeable that the lowest notes are hardly ever used. A low D makes a solitary appearance in the third movement; otherwise the lowest note is low F.

Another concerto written in the transitional period from the Baroque to the Classical eras is the Concerto for Bassoon and Orchestra by Johann Wilhelm Hertel (1727–89). More demanding in every respect is the concerto by Wolfgang Amadeus Mozart, to which we will return later. Together with the Concerto for Bassoon by Carl Maria von Weber (also discussed further on), it is one of the most widely performed pieces for solo bassoon. In

153

Concertstück für Oboe.

The first edition of a concert piece for oboe and orchestra by August Klughardt (1847–1902) with piano reduction.

1813 Weber also wrote an Andante and Rondo Ungarese in C minor, Op. 35, a work originally written for viola and orchestra in 1809.

Johann Wenzeslaus Kalliwoda, who, as we have seen, also wrote a virtuoso work for the oboe, composed a set of Variations and a Rondo for Bassoon and Orchestra, Op. 57. Compared to the oboe concerto this has a lower degree of difficulty, though the extremely high register is noticeable. The last of the variations for bassoon poses considerable difficulties with regard to embouchure because the player is required to perform rapid quaver leaps.

Richard Strauss also wrote a solo work for bassoon in the last year of his life – the Duet Concertino for clarinet and bassoon with strings and harp, which was composed in 1948. It is heard all too infrequently in concerts and on the radio.

154

Excerpt from the solo part of the bassoon concerto in B flat.

Johann Christian Bach (1735–1782)

The beginning of the solo part of the bassoon concerto K 191.

Wolfgang Amadeus Mozart (1756–1791)

NINE

Famous Oboists – Then and Now

France

From the time that it was established, in 1793, the Paris Conservatoire has been an institution of central importance for French oboe playing, and remains so today. The first professor was Antoine Sallantin (1754–1816), who was a member of the Opéra orchestra from 1773 to 1813. From 1790 to 1792 he lived in London, where he studied with Johann Christian Fischer. Sallantin's most important pupil was Auguste-Gustave Vogt (1781–1871), a native of Strasbourg who was an oboist in Napoleon's *Garde* and took part in the German campaign of 1805–6. Thereafter he became principal oboe with the Opéra Comique (and later with the Opéra), and succeeded his teacher as professor at the Conservatoire. He was on good terms with the Triébert family (who have already been mentioned), and it was at his suggestion that Triébert constructed a baritone oboe. Berlioz often refers to him in his writings.

Like his predecessors, Stanislaus Verroust (1814–63) won the first prize at the Conservatoire (1834); he succeeded his teacher Vogt to the professorship in 1853. Charles-Louis Triébert (1810–67), the eldest son of the founder of the firm, Guillaume Triébert, was also a pupil of Vogt, winning the Conservatoire first prize as early as 1829. Although a co-owner of the family firm, he preferred to pursue a career as a soloist, and initially played in various French orchestras. In 1863 he was appointed to the professorship at the Conservatoire, a post he held until his death. He was followed by the oboist Felix-Charles Berthelémy (1829–68), who died a year after taking over the post.

Charles-Joseph Colin (1832–81) won the first prize for the oboe at the age of 20; a year later the harmony and accompaniment prize, and at the age of 22 the organ prize. In 1857 he competed for the Rome Prize and came second. The Rome prize was of the greatest importance for the career of a composer: Hector Berlioz, who failed to win it twice, was finally awarded it at the third attempt. At the age of 36 Colin was appointed to the Conservatoire professorship, a post he retained until he died.

His successor was George Gillet (1854–1934), who was only 27 at the time, having won the first prize at the Conservatoire at the early age of 15. Before going to the Conservatoire he was principal oboe in concerts given by the Opéra Comique, and at the Opéra. The plateaux system of the French oboe, also called system no.6 by Triébert, bears his name to this day. After Gillet, who retired from the professorship at the age of 75, the post went to L-F-A Bleuzet (1874–1941). His successor was Pierre Bajeux.

Five oboists who were trained at the Conservatoire, though they did not become professors, remain to be mentioned. The first of these is Joseph-François Garnier (1759–1825), who was a pupil of Sallantin and an excellent teacher and concert soloist. His *Méthode de Hautbois* (c 1800) appeared in French and German editions and was favourably received in both countries. (At that time the training of oboists in the two countries was not as different as it was subsequently to become.)

Appollon Marie-Rose Barret (1804–79) was a pupil of Vogt. In 1850 he published (in English) *A Complete Method for the Oboe*. With the help of a special thumb-plate for b flat' and c'' he modified Triébert's system no.5, which nowadays, particularly in English-speaking countries, is known as the 'thumb-plate' system. It is very popular, for some passages are in fact easier to play using this system, e.g. the A minor broken chord. Lavigne and Barret were two of a number of French oboists who had a profound influence on the English school. As early as 1829 the latter was playing at Covent Garden in London, where he remained until 1874. In the second edition of his tutor, which appeared in 1862, he described the key system he had developed. Like Barret, Antoine-Joseph Lavigne (1816–86) was a pupil of

Pierre Pierlot has received many awards for his recordings. He is the most famous representative of the French school of oboe playing. Photo: RCA, Hamburg.

Vogt. He worked in England from 1841 onwards, and in 1861 became a member of the famous Hallé Orchestra in Manchester. Lavigne was particularly interested in applying the Boehm system to the oboe, which he continued to champion.

Louis Bas should also be mentioned in this connection. His biography remains unclear, though he wrote a tutor that was widely used in France – *Methode Nouvelle de Hautbois*. Today Pierre Pierlot is perhaps the most famous French oboist. With the flautist Jean-Pierre Rampal he founded the *Ensemble Baroque de Paris*, which has played all over the world. He is principal oboe with the Paris Opéra Comique, editor of the *Collection Pierre Pierlot* series, and has made many records. The conductor Harry Halbreich has paid this tribute to the unique quality of his playing:

158

(He) ennobles everything he performs with a unique tone quality, with a synthesis of magic and austerity, gracefulness and emotion, rustic freshness and humour.

Germany

Here we must begin by mentioning the Barth family. Christian Samuel Barth (1735–1809), who was a pupil at the St Thomas School in Leipzig under Johann Sebastian Bach, went to Weimar as chamber musician in 1762, and had the same post in Hanover from 1768 onwards. Shortly afterwards he became a member of the ducal chapel in Kassel, and in 1786 moved to the Royal Society in Copenhagen. The 'celestial beauty' of his tone was universally acclaimed.

He had two sons: Friedrich Philipp Carl August Barth (1774–1804) and Christian Frederik Barth (1787–1861). The elder became a member of the Royal Chapel in Copenhagen at the age of 14, also distinguishing himself as a successful composer for the oboe. The younger brother also became a member of the Copenhagen orchestra (at the age of 15) and later undertook extended concert tours. One of his pupils was Christian Schiemann (1823–1915), the author of some rather difficult virtuoso studies.

We have already mentioned Friedrich Ramm (1744–1811), who was born in Mannheim. He became a member of the Electoral Palatinate Chapel at the age of 14, remaining in this post all his life, although no less a person than Frederick William II of Prussia (1744–97) attempted to secure his services. Concert tours took him all over Europe. Mozart met Ramm in Mannheim and wrote the quartet for oboe, violin, viola and cello K370 for him. Later Ramm often played Mozart's concerto for oboe and orchestra K314 (*see p. 145*). He is mentioned in Mozart's letters

The first of the Seven Characteristic Studies.

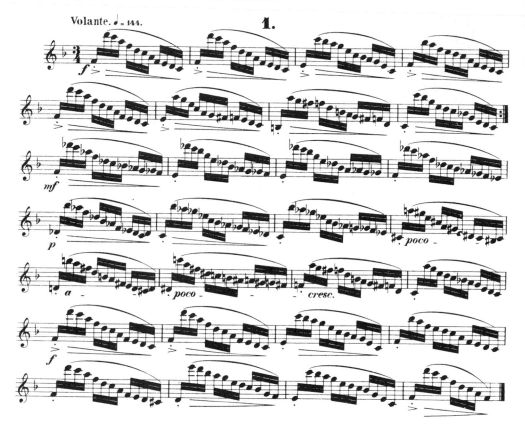

on a number of occasions in a way that enables us to deduce that they were close friends.

Jakob Alexander Lebrun came from Brussels. From 1747 until his death in 1771 he was oboist and repetiteur at the Electoral Court in Mannheim. His son Ludwig August (1752–90) became a member of the Court Orchestra at the age of 14, being appointed Court Musician in 1767. Within a short space of time he became one of the most famous oboe virtuosos of his age, enchanting the whole of Paris, as the poet Christian Friedrich Daniel Schubart (1739–91) tells us, with his heavenly playing. In 1778 he married the singer Franziska Danzi (1756–91), and toured the whole of Europe with her. To the end of his life he remained in the service of the Bavarian-Palatinate court. Towards the end of his career his salary amounted to the princely sum of 1500 gulden a year. Lebrun also composed a series of oboe concertos and chamber music for wind.

Wolfgang Amadeus Mozart (1756–91).
Silhouette by Hieronymus Löschenkohl (1785)

The Braun family of musicians is of particular interest in that most of its members were oboists, and that they attempted to develop a style of their own. The founder of the family, Anton Braun (1729–98), probably came to Kassel in 1742, initially working as regimental oboist and later playing the violin as Court Musician. He took a keen interest in the education of his eldest son, Johann Braun, and for this reason was granted an annual education allowance of 50 thalers from the Court Treasury from 1763 onwards. Johann Friedrich Braun (1759–1824) was a pupil of Christian Samuel Barth (*see above*), though he was later sent to Dresden to study with Carlo Besozzi at the landgrave's expense. In 1777 Braun became oboist and violinist in Ludwigslust, marrying the daughter of the Court Kapellmeister in 1786. Concert tours also took Johann Friedrich Braun to Hamburg (1784) and elsewhere. Josef Sittard's *Geschichte des Musik- und Concertwesens in Hamburg vom vierzehnten Jahrhundert bis auf die Gegenwart* tells us:

> Of the famous oboists who played in Hamburg in the last century we must name Johann Friedrich Braun (1784), Ludwig August Lebrun (1790), Christian Samuel Barth (1806) and Wilhelm Braun, the son of Johann Friedrich, who performed in a concert of the Harmonie in the year 1827.

Johann Friedrich Braun was above all concerned to achieve a synthesis of the expressive manner of Barth and the virtuoso brilliance of Besozzi. Karl Anton Philipp Braun (1788–1835) was already giving concerts at the age of 18, and became Danish Chamber Musician in Copenhagen in 1807. In 1815 he was called to Stockholm to become a member of the Court Orchestra, later becoming director of music of the local regiments.

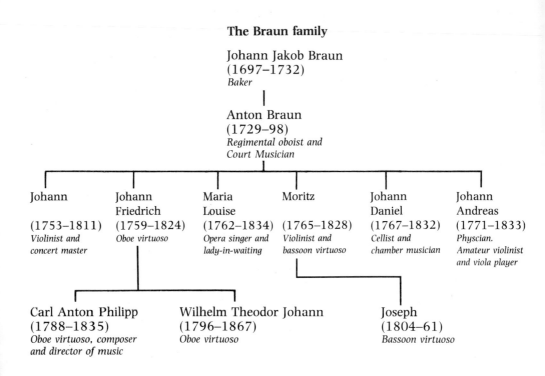

The Braun family

Johann Jakob Braun
(1697–1732)
Baker

Anton Braun
(1729–98)
*Regimental oboist and
Court Musician*

Johann	Johann Friedrich	Maria Louise	Moritz	Johann Daniel	Johann Andreas
(1753–1811)	(1759–1824)	(1762–1834)	(1765–1828)	(1767–1832)	(1771–1833)
Violinist and concert master	*Oboe virtuoso*	*Opera singer and lady-in-waiting*	*Violinist and bassoon virtuoso*	*Cellist and chamber musician*	*Physcian. Amateur violinist and viola player*

Carl Anton Philipp
(1788–1835)
*Oboe virtuoso, composer
and director of music*

Wilhelm Theodor Johann
(1796–1867)
Oboe virtuoso

Joseph
(1804–61)
Bassoon virtuoso

Johann Friedrich's second son, Wilhelm Theodor Johann Braun (1796–1867), was also an oboe virtuoso, and secured a post in Berlin in his youth. Yet with Wilhelm Theodor Johann Braun the era of oboe virtuosos reached its end, and at about this time the court orchestras began to go into decline. Moritz Braun's son Joseph Braun (1804–61) was a bassoon virtuoso and worked as Chamber Musician in Donaueschingen. He also undertook several concert tours. The pieces he played were typical of his time: they have names such as *Souvenir de Donaueschingen, Dramatic Sketch on a cantilena by Bellini*, etc.

Beginning of the Sonata for Bassoon and Violoncello K 292.

Wolfgang Amadeus Mozart (1756–1791)

Bassoon

Violoncello

We must also mention Joseph Sellner, whose oboe tutor became very famous both in France and Germany. From 1811 to 1817 Sellner was principal oboe at the theatre in Prague under Carl Maria von Weber (1786–1826). Later he went to Vienna and became a member of the Court Chapel. Sellner already played on an oboe with 13 keys (for which his tutor is written). In 1821 he became professor at the Vienna Conservatory, where, in 1825, he published his oboe tutor. The Sellner oboe was developed in collaboration with the Viennese instrument maker Stephan Koch (1772–1828); it was the forerunner of the modern Viennese oboe.

At the beginning of the twentieth century there were no great oboe virtuosos in Germany, though a new generation of players arose under the leadership of Fritz Flemming. Flemming studied in Paris between 1890 and 1891, and was appointed to the post of professor at the Berlin Hochschule in 1907. He had a lasting influence on Richard Strauss, who mentioned him in the *Instrumentationslehre*. The introduction of French fingering goes back to him; many composers had complained vociferously about the German oboe tone. Strauss's commentary on Berlioz's *Traité d'Instrumentation* is famous; we quote what he had to say on the oboe in full:

> With its thick and impudent low notes and its thin tailor-like piercing high register the oboe, especially when it is played in an exaggerated manner, is particularly suited to humorous effects and to caricature. The oboe can rasp, bleat and screech just as much as it can sing and wail in a noble and chaste way, and play and pipe in a blithe, childish manner.

Later generations of oboists were trained by the Lauschmann brothers, of whom Richard Lauschmann (1889–1980) is best known. He appeared frequently as a soloist. From 1918 onwards

Contemporary music for the same combination.

Albrecht Gürsching (1934)

Bassoon

Violoncello

he played in the Kiel City Orchestra, and did much to encourage the publication of old oboe concertos. The cor anglais by Jacques Albert in Brussels depicted on page 103, no. 4, comes from his collection, Hermann Töttcher also belongs to this generation. He favoured a bright Mönnig boxwood oboe, with which he made numerous recordings. A similar boxwood oboe by G. Urban (Hamburg) is depicted on page 83, no. 2.

Helmut Winschermann (b. 1920) has trained many of the oboists who now play in German orchestras. He studied the oboe in Essen and in Paris. After completing his studies he worked as a soloist before taking over the master class at the Music Academy in Detmold in 1951. In 1956 he was appointed to the post of professor. He also directs various chamber music ensembles.

Among the musicians who not only have complete command over their instrument but who are also interested in the history of music is Georg Meerwein (b. 1932), principal oboe with the Bamberg Symphony Orchestra. He has undertaken many tours with this orchestra, has given master classes in Germany and abroad, and has made a name for himself with his articles, broadcasts and essays.

Ingo Goritzki (b. 1939) won various national and international competitions and was appointed professor at the Hochschule in Hannover in 1972. Apart from numerous recordings and concerts he has written articles on the history and the repertoire of his instrument.

Albrecht Gürsching (b. 1934) studied the oboe and composition in Detmold and Munich. Since 1964 he has been professor for oboe, woodwind chamber music, theory and composition at the Hochschule in Hamburg. He has undertaken numerous tours at home and abroad. Among his works we should single out two oboe concertos, a bassoon concerto and some woodwind chamber music (*see the accompanying music example*).

164

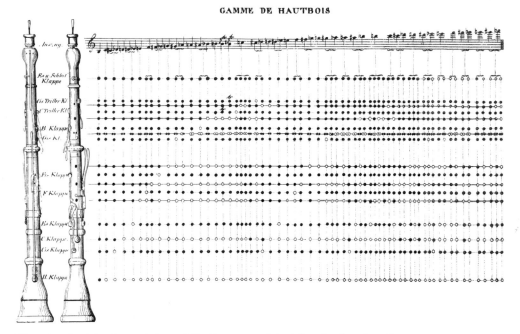

Fingering chart for the prototype of the German and Austrian oboe based on the ideas of Sellner and incorporating improvements by Foreith. (Caecilia IV. Schott. Mainz, 1826.) See also page 68–69.

If one may speak of a North German school of oboe playing at all, then Heinz Nordbruch (b. 1921) is its most significant representative. In contrast to the South German and the French concept of tone, the North German orchestras prefer a particularly soft and dark oboe tone which is achieved by using hard reeds with long tables and instruments with thicker walls. The Püchner (Nauheim) model oboe was first able to gain acceptance here. Heinz Nordbruch became principal oboe with the Bremen Radio Orchestra at the age of 18, and in 1948 was appointed to the same post at the North German Radio Symphony Orchestra. Since 1964 he has taught at the Hochschule in Hamburg, and was appointed professor in 1974.

Austria

The Vienna school of woodwind playing[68] can be traced back to Joseph Sellner, who played under Carl Maria von Weber in Prague, and then became a member of the Court Chapel in Vienna, where, in 1821, he was appointed Professor for Oboe at

165

ORCHESTERSTUDIEN
FÜR
HOBOE UND **ENGLISCH HORN**
AUS
RICHARD STRAUSS'
SYMPHONISCHEN WERKEN

I. II.

AUSGEWÄHLT UND
BEZEICHNET VON
RICH. BRUMGÄRTEL

AUFFÜHRUNGSRECHT VORBEHALTEN
"UNIVERSAL-EDITION"
AKTIENGESELLSCHAFT
WIEN — LEIPZIG
COPYRIGHT 1910 BY UNIVERSAL-EDITION

the Conservatory. One of the most important of Sellner's successors was Richard Baumgärtel (1858–1941), a native of Dresden, who joined the Vienna Opera in 1880. From Dresden Baumgärtel brought the much sought-after oboes of Carl Golde (d. 1873), which at the time were the most modern instruments in the whole of Germany. The Golde firm of woodwind instrument makers was carried on by father and son – the latter took his own life at his father's grave. Baumgärtel improved this model with the help of the Viennese instrument maker Joseph Hajek (1849–1926).

This instrument was adopted by Alexander Wunderer (1877–1955), who played with the Vienna Philharmonic from 1900 to 1932. Subsequently Hajek and his successor Hermann Zuleger (1885–1949) made further modifications to the Viennese oboe at the behest of Professor Hans Hadamowsky (1906–86), and in this form it is still played by the Vienna Philharmonic today. Yet even in Austria the use of the Viennese oboe is declining, for the students of the Vienna Academy can only play in a few orchestras if they learn to play the Viennese oboe – a problem similar to that experienced by French bassoonists.

Switzerland

When one reads of the worldwide successes which Heinz Holliger has achieved with his oboe playing one is reminded of the reports of the early oboe virtuosos in the eighteenth century. Holliger was born in 1939 in Langenthal in Switzerland. While still at high school he studied at the Berne Conservatory, where his oboe teacher was Emile Cassagnaud and his composition teacher Sándor Veress. Like many other oboe players before him he completed his studies in Paris, because the French place particular emphasis on virtuoso playing, in contrast to the German school, where tonal and expressive qualities are more important than polished technique. In Paris his teacher was Pierre Pierlot. He also studied composition in Basle with Pierre Boulez (b. 1925). He was awarded numerous prizes at international competitions, and has performed with almost all of the leading orchestras.

Heinz Holliger plays with a hitherto unknown brilliance, which he couples with a polished breathing technique. It hardly needs to be said that he commands the technique of circular breathing. He can also be compared to earlier generations of oboists in that he has made a name for himself as a composer (not only of oboe music). His *Mobiles* for oboe and harp (1962), which he wrote for himself and his wife, a well-known harpist, are characteristic of his style. A whole row of contemporary composers has been inspired by his playing to compose oboe concertos, including Ernst Krenek, Klaus Huber, Sándor Veress, Henri Pousseur, André Jolivet, Krzysztof Penderecki and Hans Werner Henze. In his capacity as professor for the oboe at the

167

The virtuoso playing of the Swiss oboist Heinz Holliger has popularized the oboe and its music. Photo: Polygram Hamburg.

Musikhochschule in Freiburg im Breisgau, he has already trained a number of pupils who have also achieved fame. One of them is Thomas Indermühle (b. 1951 in Berne), a prize winner at the international oboe competition in Prague in 1974. He became principal oboe with the Netherlands Chamber Orchestra in Amsterdam in the same year.

England

We have already mentioned the founders of the English school, Johann Christian Fischer and Appollon Barret. In our century Leon Goossens has attained an almost legendary reputation.

168

Some of the experiences of his remarkable 60-year career as a teacher, an orchestral musician and a soloist are preserved in a book entitled *Oboe* that he wrote jointly with the oboist and composer Edwin Roxburgh. It appeared in 1977 in the Yehudi Menuhin Music Guides series. Leon Goossens was born in 1897, and was professor both at the Royal College of Music and the Royal Academy of Music in London. His career as a soloist has taken him to Europe, to the United States, to Canada, to Australia and to the Soviet Union.

Evelyn Rothwell (b. 1911) was a pupil of Goossens. In 1939 she married the conductor Sir John Barbirolli. In addition to publishing some sets of orchestral studies she wrote a book, *Oboe Technique*, from which oboists can still learn much. Janet Craxton (1929–81) was professor at the Royal Academy of Music, and principal oboe of the Hallé Orchestra and BBC Symphony Orchestra. She made a number of recordings and published two volumes of solo oboe music. Malcolm Messiter (b. 1949) is a gifted oboist whose virtuosity is striking. He only began to play the oboe at the age of 15, and later studied briefly with Pierre Pierlot in Paris.

Nowadays it is no longer unusual to find women among the woodwind group of a symphony orchestra. Our photo shows Jane Bennett on the second desk of the Bournemouth Symphony Orchestra.

Mobile 3 for oboe and harp.

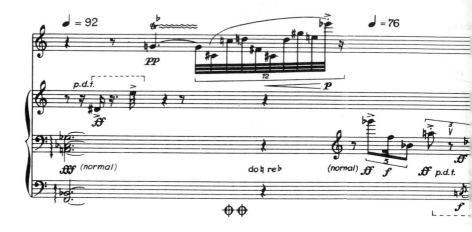

Spain

The Spanish school is mentioned here mainly because it represents a serious attempt to introduce the Boehm system. Pierre Joachim Raimond Soler (1810–50) was trained in Paris, winning the first prize in 1836, and subsequently working as an oboist in the orchestra of the Opéra Comique. He was an enthusiastic disciple of the Boehm system, and managed to enlist the interest of the Madrid teacher and oboist Enrique Marzo, who in 1870 produced a tutor with fingering charts for the Boehm system oboe.[69] Marzo and Soler obviously had an influence on South America, where the Boehm instrument made some headway. This is suggested by the existence of Boehm oboes in South American countries. An instrument of this kind stamped by Weril of São Paulo in Brazil is depicted on page 82.

Soviet Union

According to a report by James A. MacGillivray in the *Journal of the Galpin Society*, many oboes of the German type were still being used in Russia in 1956. They had been made before the First World War by Julius Heinrich Zimmermann, whose headquarters were in Leipzig, but who had branches in St Petersburg, Moscow, Riga and London, and whose reputation rested on his wind and string instruments. Nowadays many instruments of the French type are probably being used, most of them of East German origin. A recording from the Soviet Union available in West Germany depicts an oboe on the sleeve with a maker's mark in Cyrillic letters (which are shown the wrong way round). This is doubtless an oboe of the French type. The soloist on this

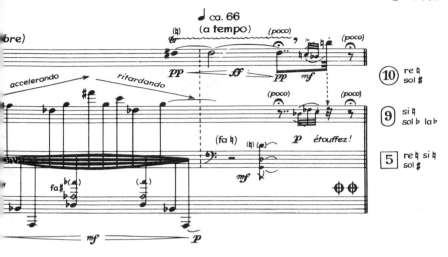

recording, Juosas Rimas (b. 1942), is principal oboe with the Vilna orchestra and teaches a class for wind ensembles at the local conservatory. (The photo with the oboe was taken in the art gallery in Vilna.)

United States

One of the most important American oboists was Josef Marx (1913–78), who had a great reputation both as an oboist and as a musicologist. Born in Berlin, he studied in Paris with Marcel Dandois and in London with Leon Goossens. Before the Second World War he went to New York, where in 1946 he founded the music publishing firm of MacGinnis & Marx, which issues books on music and music for the oboe. Josef Marx also played an important role in the rediscovery of old music. As early as 1951 he wrote a much-admired essay on the tone of the Baroque oboe for the *Journal of the Galpin Society*.

Ray Still is considered to be one of the best North American oboists. He graduated from the Julliard School in 1947 and in 1954 became solo oboist of the Chicago Symphony Orchestra and professor at Northwestern University. He has played concertos under Fritz Reiner and George Solti, and oboe quartets with the Julliard, Vermeer and Fine Arts Quartets.

Bruce Haynes (b. 1942) is a specialist in Baroque oboes. A pupil of the recorder virtuoso Frans Brüggen, Haynes plays the Baroque oboe and the recorder, and has taught both at the Royal Conservatory in The Hague since 1972. He has published several articles on the Baroque oboe (reed making) and has compiled a comprehensive bibliography of oboe chamber music.

171

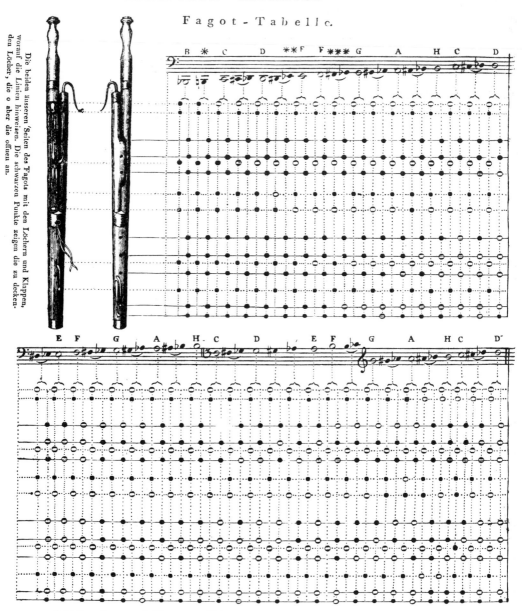

'Fagot-Fabelle' from the rare German translation of the famous Bassoon-tutor of Etienne Ozi (1753)–1813), Leipzig 1806.

TEN

Famous Bassoonists – Then and now

France

Both flautists and bassoonists can lay claim to an eminent composer: François Devienne (1759–1803). In 1787 he performed a Symphonie Concertante for flute, clarinet and bassoon; and in 1789 he became principal bassoon at the Théâtre de Monsieur, retaining this post until his death. Devienne wrote a large number of pieces for the flute and for the bassoon, as well as for other wind instruments such as the clarinet, the horn and the oboe. François-René Gebauer (1773–1845), a pupil of Devienne, became the first teacher of the bassoon at the Paris Conservatoire at the early age of 22. From 1801 to 1826 he also played the bassoon at the Paris Opéra.

Gebauer took over a bassoon tutor written by Etienne Ozi (1754–1813) – the most famous bassoon tutor apart from that of Weissenborn. Gebauer's successor was Friedrich Berr (1794–1838), who achieved fame both as a clarinet and a bassoon virtuoso. Berr played no small part in the reorganization of French military music, and in 1836 was appointed director of the new School of Military Music. He wrote a tutor for the clarinet with 14 keys (1836) and a bassoon tutor. Of the many famous French bassoonists we should mention Fernand Oubradous, who was born in 1903. Initially a bassoonist, he subsequently studied composition at the Paris Conservatory and was later active as a composer and conductor.

Germany

The history of the bassoon as a solo instrument was never very spectacular, for it tended to be put in the shade by the oboe, as in the case of the Besozzi brothers from Turin. The Braun family also produced two good bassoonists. Yet, compared with the oboists,

First edition of Friedrich Berr's (1794–1838) arrangement for bassoon and piano of the 'Cavatine' from Gioacchino Rossini's opera The Thieving Magpie.

travelling bassoonists were few and far between, and a whole row of bassoon concertos was written at the instigation of amateurs. Thus we owe to Freiherr Thaddeus von Dürnitz (d. 1803) the only surviving bassoon concerto by Mozart. There are said to have been three others, but they are considered lost. The most significant bassoon concerto after the Mozart is probably the one by Carl Maria von Weber, which was written in 1811. The manuscript of the work has survived and carries the name of the man who commissioned it. It is entitled 'Concerto per il Fagotto Principale composto per uso dell Signore Brandt da Carlo Maria de Weber'. Weber recorded the exact details of the work's creation in his diary:

174

Munich, 1811
  14 Nov. Adagio comp. in Brandt's concerto
  17 Nov. Rondo for Brandt completed
  26 Nov. Allegro for Brandt completed
  27 Nov. Scored bassoon rondo

Georg Friedrich Brandt (1773–1836) was 'First Royal Court Musician on the Bassoon' from 1800 onwards, and achieved fame on account of numerous concert tours. We do not know when he first played Weber's concerto, but from the *Leipziger Allgemeine Musik-Zeitung* we know that he performed it in Prague in 1813. It was written for an instrument with only a few keys which did not as yet incorporate the improvements of Almenräder and Heckel. In 1822 Weber revised the work – a sign that he attached some importance to it.

The importance of Carl Almenräder as an improver of the bassoon has already been mentioned. In addition Almenräder was also an important bassoon virtuoso, joining the Cologne Theatre Orchestra as early as 1810. Later he went to Frankfurt and, in 1816, to the 34th Regiment of the Line in Mainz. In 1817 he moved to the State Theatre as a bassoonist, and at the same time conducted his experiments on how to improve the bassoon in the Schott workshops. It was here that he came across his later partner Johann Adam Heckel. His tutor *Die Kunst des Fagott-Blasens, Méthode complète de Basson* appeared in 1843.

His music is closely bound up with his instrument, and he wrote a work in the increasingly popular genre of variations on a theme: *Introduction et Variations sur le thème "Es eilen die Stunden des Lebens so schnell dahin!" pour le basson avec acc. de violon, viola et violoncelle* Op. 4 (1827). His compositions make full use of all the capabilities inherent in the bassoon and betray his profound musicianship.

Excerpt from Act 1 of Die Walküre *by Richard Wagner (1813–83). The old stranger to whom Sieglinde refers is her father Wotan. At 'Mässig' the entry of the Valhalla motif in the horns and bassoons discloses his true identity in musical terms. In the third bassoon the 'Wagner bell' is required for the low A.*

More famous than this and still in use today is the tutor by Christian Julius Weissenborn (1837–88). Weissenborn was principal bassoon with the Gewandhaus Orchestra in Leipzig and taught at the local conservatory. His practical bassoon tutor also became known overseas, was translated into English and has gone through numerous editions. As a composer Weissenborn wrote music mainly for his own instrument. The six pieces for three bassoons, Op. 4, are particularly charming. They are subtitled as follows:

1 Serenade
2 The first ball with the loved one
3 *Thé dansant* in the small country palace
4 Dance in the village inn
5 The soldiers of the watch parade at midnight
6 The last hour of a humourist

Like Carl Almenräder, Reinhold Lange in Wiesbaden was interested in the bassoon both as a player and as an instrument maker. He was born in 1854 and died in 1905. We know that he was active as a maker from 1892 onwards. Around this time he published *Abhandlung über die Verbesserungen des Fagottes* (Treatise concerning improvements to the bassoon), which carried Almenräder's ideas a step further. His bassoons were fairly popular, and were rather unwelcome competition for the firm of Heckel in the Wiesbaden suburb of Biebrich. On page 91, no. 3 we depict a bassoon by Reinhold Lange which, in addition to the normal bell for the low B flat, possesses a second, longer bell for the low A (also known as 'Wagner bell'). It is required in those instances in *Die Walküre* where the bassoon has to descend to the low A.

Wilhelm Heinitz (1883–1963) is an example of a bassoonist who later became a scholar. Initially principal bassoon in orchestras at home and abroad, he later became an assistant in the phonetics laboratory of the Seminar for African and South Sea Languages at the University of Hamburg. Here he subsequently founded the research unit for comparative musicology. In this connection we should mention his volume on instruments in *Handbuch der Musikwissenschaft*, which appeared in 1929.

England

At the beginning of the nineteenth century English music was greatly influenced by French musicians. A famous bassoonist at this time was Friedrich Baumann (1801–56). Born at Ostende, he was awarded the first prize at the Paris Conservatory in 1822, after which he went to England. He played in various orchestras, and also appeared with Barret. However, when Hans Richter (1843–1916) became conductor of the Hallé Orchestra he insisted on the introduction of German-system bassoons, and to this end engaged two Viennese basoonists to play in his orchestra. Otto Schieder (d. 1950) became professor at the Royal Manchester College of Music and trained the first generation of English bassoonists on the German instrument.

This generation included Archie Camden (1888–1979), who succeeded his teacher in the Hallé Orchestra and at the Royal Manchester College of Music. He later played in the BBC Symphony Orchestra and was much in demand as a soloist. He also wrote a book entitled *Bassoon Technique*, to which the English

Famous Bassoonists – Then and Now

Caricature of the bassoonist Milan Turković by his Concentus Musicus colleague Walter Pfeiffer.

The Melos Ensemble playing Ludwig van Beethoven's (1770–1827) Septet Op. 20. From left to right: Emanuel Hurwitz (violin), Neil Sanders (horn), Gervase de Peyer (clarinet), William Waterhouse (bassoon), Cecil Aronowitz (viola), Adrian Beers (double bass) and Terence Weil (violoncello). Photos: Auerbach, London.

A concert in Brighton Pavilion, which was built for George IV (1762–1830). Oboes and bassoons play important roles in woodwind chamber music, which is heard all too infrequently. Sometimes the cor anglais and the double bassoon are also required. Photo: Auerbach, London.

179

bassoonist William R. Waterhouse (b. 1931) contributed a bibliography of bassoon literature. Like Archie Camden before him, Waterhouse plays in the BBC Symphony Orchestra, and collects old bassoons. He is the author of the New Grove article on the bassoon, has edited numerous works for the instrument (he is one of the editors of *Universal Bassoon Edition*), and has described his important collection of bassoons in *The Proud Bassoon* (Edinburgh, 1983).

Austria

Many bassoonists from Europe and overseas have studied with Karl Oehlberger (b. 1912) at the Vienna Academy of Music. He began to study the bassoon in 1930 with Professor Karl Strobel, his predecessor in this post, graduating in 1936 and becoming principal bassoon with the Vienna State Opera and the Vienna Philharmonic. In 1938 he was appointed to the post of professor at the Academy of Music – which he holds to this day.

Milan Turković belongs to the younger generation of bassoonists. Born in Zagreb in 1939, he was also a pupil of Karl Oehlberger, later completing his studies with Albert Hennige (Detmold) and Sol Schoenbach (Philadelphia). From 1962 to 1967 he was principal bassoon of the Bamberg Symphony Orchestra and a member of the Bamberg Wind Quintet. Thereafter he became principal bassoon with the Vienna Philharmonic. Today he teaches at the Mozarteum in Salzburg.

This brief survey of some of the most important oboists and bassoonists is of course not intended to be an exhaustive list, and for reasons of space some important names have been omitted. The reader is referred to Lyndesay G. Langwill, *The Bassoon and Contrabassoon* (London, 1971), and Will Jansen, *The Bassoon* (Buren, Holland, 1978).

ELEVEN

Advice for Beginners

Learning the Oboe

Today more and more amateurs are taking up the oboe, whereas a few years ago it was almost exclusively played by professional musicians. Learning the instrument was said to involve insuperable problems for the layman. There was the problem of reeds, which was considered impossible to overcome; of the compressed air, which was said to lead to an enlargement of the lungs or to physical deformation on account of the pressure on the brain (is the skull not rooted firmly on the spine, one asks oneself?); and there was talk of other incredible difficulties. For example, it was thought that musicians could only play the oboe up to the age of 40.

Many of these things belong to the realm of fiction. Yet prejudices, as we all know, die hard. I once had the following experience. While I was a young musician in the Army I sometimes suffered from headaches – the result of having to play a lot of marches, which, as every oboist knows, is in fact the most strenuous activity there is, apart from Handel's oratorios or the works of Bach. For this reason I went to the sickbay in the barracks in which the band was stationed, reported to the doctor on duty and was finally admitted to his presence.

'Aha,' said the doctor, mustering the white facings with a knowing look, 'so you're a musician?.'
　'Yes, sir.'
　'What's your instrument?'
　'I play the oboe.'
　'Well, what's the matter?'
　'I keep having headaches.'
Turning to the orderly, the doctor, said:
　'Give this man a large supply of painkillers. Oboists all go mad in the end anyway.'

So much for the doctor. I usually counter such remarks by replying, 'Quite right, but the good thing is that one doesn't notice it oneself'. (Of course, I didn't dare to say it on this occasion.).

In the specialist literature at any rate there is nothing to suggest that the pressure which accumulates in the oral cavity has an effect on the brain. Brass players have to cope with much higher air pressure levels. A neurologist I have consulted on this point has heard of no case of an oboist whose brain has been damaged in this way. Yet the idea dies hard, and the occasional sideways glance of ostensibly well-informed fellow human beings seems to corroborate the fact that this is a prejudice oboists will simply have to live with.

It is true that even a few decades ago people used much harder reeds, and that the effort expended when playing the oboe, at least to judge by films and television recordings of concerts, must have been greater. Even today the older generation of oboists has to and obviously wishes to play with much harder reeds than younger musicians are used to. But then amateur oboists should not really use hard reeds, for they are not in a position to practise their instrument for hours every day, and thus cannot strengthen the lip muscles to the point where they can cope with them. Reeds that are too hard usually lead to intonation and response problems; and then of course the other players in amateur orchestras will start to complain about the bad intonation in the oboe section (despite the fact that this is usually also in evidence in the other woodwind groups).

Nowadays more and more young people are displaying an interest in the oboe, and girls in particular are often keen on learning an instrument which has wrongly been regarded as 'difficult'. Those who decide to take up the oboe are usually interested in classical music, for it so happens that the oboe is

Gerard Hoffnung (1925–59) Oboist. (Munich, Vienna. Verlag Langen-Müller.)

Beginners will not get tired so easily if they select light oboe reeds.

mainly used in Baroque, in so-called classical or in serious music. There have been repeated attempts to make use of the oboe in jazz combinations, but these have never got very far, and the oboe, though a welcome guest, is rarely used in folk music on account of the expense involved.

Once you have decided to play the oboe you should always proceed as follows. If you are lucky enough to be at a school which is able to lend you an instrument, getting started should be fairly easy. Yet school instruments are frequently in a state of disrepair, often because the authorities have thought fit to buy the cheapest instruments on the market. Pupils and teachers then have to struggle with an oboe whose sound and intonation leave a lot to be desired. But you will get off to a good start by seeking the advice of a teacher right from the beginning. Learning the oboe on one's own is not a good idea, and the mistakes which you are likely to make in this way (and which one can occasionally observe in the case of amateurs) are many. Wrong breathing technique, faulty posture, reeds that are too hard, instruments that are not properly regulated – these are just a few of the things that can go wrong.

Gerard Hoffnung (1925–59): Lady bassoonist.
(Munich, Vienna, Verlag Langen-Müller.)

Learning the Bassoon

If you decide in favour of the bassoon you should bear in mind that, even more than in the case of the oboe, your musical activities will tend to be restricted to the sphere of what is commonly referred to as classical music.

The last few years have seen the publication of some interesting works for bassoon, and new editions of Renaissance and medieval music also provide interesting material – many amateur bassoonists later buy a dulcian or Baroque bassoon in order to be able to play in early music ensembles. Of course, these pieces can also be played on modern instruments. The bassoonist will naturally find plenty to do in Baroque music, for practically every continuo part can be played on the bassoon. Amateur orchestras are always on the look-out for bassoonists, and playing in school orchestras or amateur groups after one or two years of instruction should not prove too difficult.

Nowadays even ten-year-olds are starting to play the bassoon, and making good progress. When learning an instrument of this kind with all its difficulties it helps if one has the support of one's parents. A few words of encourgement are often required when things do not seem to be progressing as they should. Holding the instrument causes problems at the beginning, though a hand rest for the right hand, and if need be a special balance attachment for the left hand helps to overcome them.

For this reason it is important to practise regularly, so that hand and body posture become second nature, and, above all, in order to develop the embouchure. As in the case of the oboe, players nowadays tend to favour a relatively low pressure embouchure. The piano mechanism is now the rule, even in the case of inexpensive bassoons, and this facilitates playing in the upper octaves. It is most important that the pupil should breathe properly from the start and that he should practise abdominal

More and more people are taking up the bassoon. Jürgen Blauth (b. 1964) was one of 13 bassoonists who qualified for the eighteenth West German 'Jugend Musiziert' competition in Hamburg in 1981. Photo: Fotopress, Hamburg.

185

breathing. For this reason the pupil should always practise standing up. Without a suitable teacher – usually a musician in a municipal orchestra or a police or military band – it will prove impossible to learn the bassoon, for the pupil has to learn numerous tricks, particularly auxiliary fingering and how to cover certain holes in particular situations. In America there are tutors which claim to be able to teach the bassoon with the help of cassettes and an instruction booklet, but the cassettes are on a low musical and technical level, and you will not become a good bassoonist if you follow their advice.

Choosing a Suitable Instrument

Buying an instrument is just as difficult as choosing a good teacher. The most sensible course is to choose a teacher first and then to buy a suitable instrument with his or her help. The high cost of an oboe or a bassoon means that most people will try to buy a second-hand instrument, so here are a few hints on how to avoid making the wrong decision when buying yours.

It is always a good idea to buy an instrument that a professional musician no longer needs because he has bought himself a new one. As a rule these instruments have been played in and were carefully selected when initially purchased. In many cases, however, the condition of the instrument leaves something to be desired on account of its frequent use. If one is offered an instrument of this kind, one should pay particular attention to the following points.

Oboe

Cracks in the wood mainly come about through using a new instrument too much, through extremes of temperature or through trips to countries with very low humidity levels. The

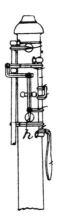

The two speaker keys on the top joint of a modern oboe. This is the place where cracks are most likely to appear. (Drawing F. Harrison patent, 1912.)

A good, relaxed posture is attained by practising standing up.

whole instrument and the top joint in particular become wet by continual exposure to the moisture in the breath, whereas the outside tends to remain dry. Thus, if an instrument is not regularly oiled, cracks caused by the tension between the two can appear on the outside. These cracks will not necessarily go right the way through immediately, but at the very least they are a warning that the instrument should be kept in an environment with balanced humidity. For this reason a woodwind instrument should not be placed near a radiator or the central heating, and it should not be placed uncleaned in its case, where it may possibly remain for days on end. The moisture remaining inside the bore cannot evaporate and, in addition to cracks, produces unsavoury hygienic conditions. (I had to clean many of the old instruments in my collection with a large household brush, and the insides with thin bottle brushes.)

A few years ago a crack could only be repaired by replacing the entire faulty joint. Nowadays, however, it is easy to seal it permanently by using epoxy resins. The old instrument makers tried to counter the possibility of cracks by strengthening the endangered parts with cross-lateral screws, though this was more usual in clarinets than in oboes. Cracks can easily appear between the speaker keys and also between the two small tone holes for the b'-c sharp' and c''-d'' trill keys. When buying an instrument one should first of all take a good look at these parts, and, if necessary, remove the speaker keys to see if there is a crack underneath them.

Cracks can best be repaired by means of headless screws and by the simultaneous use of epoxy resin. (Cracks repaired with shellac usually reopen fairly quickly, for shellac hardens, and as the wood moves they tend to reappear.) Thanks to these resilient glues one does not nowadays have to reject an instrument with a crack. The state of the mechanical parts is much more problematical: clearly, instruments of professional musicians are affected by frequent use, and their keys are often rather 'worn out', as the experts say. But if the keys are loosely attached to the rods the pads do not always fit exactly into the surrounding seatings and this can lead to leaks. In the case of instruments which have been used a lot it is often impossible to cover the tone holes properly. Yet only instruments in which the holes close perfectly (and this means that when the various parts are sucked the vacuum can be maintained for a moment) will prove really satisfying with regard to response, tone and use.

Many new instruments will probably not come up to this standard when they are delivered, and that is the reason why music shops that do not have a craftsman able to regulate the instrument rarely have an oboe one can really play. Of course, the mechanism is so complicated that even musicians who have played the oboe for years do not know exactly where the fault is located, and what one has to do in order to readjust the instrument. All this is a problem, of course, and no doubt it discourages some people from learning the oboe.

In addition to external damage – cracks and noisy mechanism – there can also be damage to the bore or the tone holes. Quite a few musicians keep making alterations to the intonation, often with rather dubious results. For the least alteration to one tone hole can mean that another note, which does not necessarily have to be an adjacent one, suddenly no longer sounds the way it should. It is a much better idea to try to overcome intonation problems by looking at the key opening and to regulate this, for key openings of different width lead to imperfect intonation. In second-hand instruments it is often the case that, if a woollen cloth has been used to clean the instrument, minute pieces of hair accumulate around the sharp edges of the bore hole rims and that these in the course of time form a constricting ring which naturally affects the tone quality. Many instruments that I have inspected and refurbished had rings of this kind, and only after they had been removed was the whole of the tone hole free once more. In most cases this overcame the imperfect intonation that had previously been a problem.

The state of the silver-plating (nickel-covered keys are sometimes found in the case of inexpensive instruments) gives an indication of the musician's cleaning habits. One should get used to polishing one's instrument with a silver-cleaning cloth immediately after one has played it. Yet most players do not do this, even though the makers' instructions make a point of telling them not to forget it. This 'sin of omission' leads to oxidization where there is no direct contact with the fingers, and sometimes to the silver-plating being worn away where the fingers touch the keys. The material underneath (today this is mostly German silver) is far less resistant to the alkaline moisture on the fingers than the silver-plating, and once this protective layer has disappeared the keywork begins to corrode.

One can see what happens by looking at old instruments in collections. Keys and rings become badly worn and when the instrument is overhauled one often has to have a new key fitted. The bore can also be damaged by breath moisture. In the case of instruments made of large-pored cocos wood, cleaning can lead to a loss of wood and thus to changes inside the bore.

This list of possible imperfections shows quite clearly that an instrument should only be selected in the presence of an expert. It is also a good idea, when buying a used instrument in need of an overhaul, to consult an instrument maker willing to give an estimate of the repair costs. Sometimes it is simply not worth buying an instrument on account of the high repair and silver-plating costs one is likely to incur.

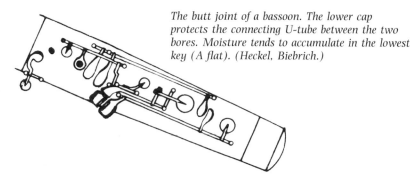

The butt joint of a bassoon. The lower cap protects the connecting U-tube between the two bores. Moisture tends to accumulate in the lowest key (A flat). (Heckel, Biebrich.)

Bassoon

The bassoon, unlike the oboe, is made of maple, not of tropical hardwood (if we are referring to the German version of the instrument – the French 'basson' is usually made of palisander rosewood), and thus it is important to make sure that the wood has not begun to rot. Nowadays many bassoonists are unfortunately of the opinion that a bassoon does not have to be wiped dry, seeing that the parts particularly exposed to moisture have a rubber lining. Few musicians seem to be aware of the fact that condensation collects at the ends of the tenons, in the sockets and on the side of the butt joint leading to the long joint, and that this quickly leads to wood decay. If the makers have not devoted enough time and care to impregnating the wood, rot can set in at these points; and this can only be avoided by cleaning the instrument regularly and thoroughly. Many pupils also fail to notice the condensation that collects in certain tone holes; at first it is only the padding which hardens on account of the moisture it absorbs, but soon the wood underneath the padding begins to rot. Closed keys (e.g. the A flat key) require particular attention in this respect.

If one is offered a used bassoon one should first of all examine the butt joint. Removing the part that connects the two tubes of the butt joint, one should examine both of them carefully. The rubber lining of the butt joint should not be damaged in any way. If it has become dull this is a sign that it has not been cleaned very often. But it is more important still to examine the side of the bore leading to the long joint and to the wing joint. Caution is called for if the wood is discoloured, if one can press one's fingernail into it easily, or if the bore is no longer round and pieces of wood have obviously broken off. In such cases wood rot has reached an advanced stage. Having these parts repaired entails taking a risk, for the rotten parts have to be gouged out, and in the process the thin dividing wall between the two tubes can easily be damaged. Subsequently the part which has been gouged out has to be covered with a rubber lining to restore the smooth bore throughout. This kind of repair work can only be carried out with a precision tool specially designed for this purpose, which only those firms which also make bassoons have at their disposal. Bassoons suffer from broken or cracked tenons more often than oboes. If for any reason a tenon is broken the rest of it has to be cut out and a new piece inserted; this is the kind of repair work which requires a great deal of experience. Cracks in the tenons can be overcome by strengthening them with metal rings.

The outside of a bassoon tends to be more easily damaged on account of the softer wood employed. In instruments that have seen a lot of use the varnish around the finger holes is frequently worn away or the bore of the tone holes is damaged. Here one can have metal shells fitted, though one must ensure that they comply exactly with the original tone hole bore, for otherwise there will be further intonation problems. In this respect the bassoon is the most sensitive of the woodwind instruments; minute alterations to the bore of the tone holes can have far-reaching consequences for the overall intonation of the instrument. Wear and tear caused by the fingers does not necessarily mean that the whole instrument has to be revarnished. Hardly a single old Italian violin still possesses all of its original layer of varnish, and yet no one would hit on the idea of stripping and revarnishing the whole instrument.

Sometimes one notices that the sound of an instrument which has been completely stripped and revarnished has changed. In such cases one tends to blame the craftsman, who, it seems, has evidently made alterations to the instrument without the owner's consent. It is easy to overlook the fact that the process of stripping the varnish naturally leads to a loss of some of the

List of production dates of Heckel bassoons based on the maker's number under the cap on the butt joint.

Year	Bassoon No.	1936	8000
1877	3000	1943	9000
1898	4000	1956	10000
1911	5000	1965	11000
1924	6000	1975	12000
1929	7000	1985	13000

underlying wood, a loss that the new layer of varnish cannot make good. (Some musicians even claim that different kinds of varnish produce different kinds of tone.) Finally, when buying a used bassoon one should try to make sure that one is buying an instrument by an established maker; this is the only way of ensuring that one is getting a good instrument whose tone, tuning and response will turn out to be satisfactory.

In the case of oboes one will therefore tend to favour the smaller firms. Once one has become acquainted with the various makes one can tell from the serial numbers when the instrument was made; alternatively, one can obtain this information by getting in touch with the makers themselves. All good instruments have an individual serial number which makes it possible to find out who the previous owners were and when they were made. Bassoons made by the firm of Heckel in Biebrich are much in demand all over the world, and a beginner will find it rather difficult to obtain an instrument of this kind immediately. Prices for used Heckel bassoons are often higher than those of new factory-made instruments, even if the instrument concerned is 20, 30 or even 50 years old. Bassoons with serial numbers between 7000 and 9000 are particularly sought after, and people are sometimes prepared to pay prices approaching those of a new Heckel bassoon for these instruments. Quite a number of bassoons made by this firm are still being played in orchestras today, even though they are 60 or 70 years old.

At the other end of the scale, instruments are now being made of synthetic materials, especially in America. They are to be recommended for beginners, for they are durable and can survive excessive use and faulty storage. However, there is little reliable information on the long-term performance and hardening of synthetic materials.

There have been repeated attempts to make instruments using

material other than wood. These include crystal glass flutes by Laurent, metal clarinets by Rott, ivory instruments for players of particular discernment, and instruments made of plexiglass, which were made in the 1930s by the firms of Mönnig and Heckel for use in the tropics. An oboe of this kind is depicted on page 83, no. 1.

Bassoons have also been made of ebonite. An instrument of this kind is depicted on page 91, no. 2. However, the additional weight brought about by the use of rubber is a disadvantage. It is precisely because oboes and bassoons are so very expensive that the beginner should buy a quality instrument. He will find it easier to learn on, and the resale value, if he later wishes to buy a better instrument, will be much higher. The fact that prices tend to keep increasing means that, in a few years' time, one can count on obtaining the price one paid oneself – if, that is, one has bought a quality instrument. It should, however, be an instrument which has been carefully cared for, and where the sort of damage indicated above has been avoided.

If someone wishes nonetheless to buy an instrument on his own he should at least be clear in his own mind about the fingering system he requires. In the case of the oboe several fingering systems are still in use today. In Germany the fully automatic Conservatoire system tends to prevail; here the two speaker keys are operated solely by means of one thumb key, whereby the upper and lower speaker keys are opened using a mechanism linked to the g'' key. In America, Britain and the Romance countries this system is usually rejected on account of its supposed unreliability; here one tends to find the semi-automatic system, in which, for notes from a'' upwards, the speaker key is operated with the ball of the left forefinger. In addition to this, the thumbplate system, as it is called, is used in Anglo-Saxon countries. This originated in France, and simplifies the notes b flat' and c''. In certain technical passages this system has its advantages, though it is sometimes difficult to find teachers who both know and are prepared to teach it.

In practice it does not matter which system the beginner learns, for he will become acquainted with all of them in the course of time, though if he begins on an instrument with automatic speaker keys and later wishes to transfer to a semi-automatic system, he will find it rather difficult to get used to the separate keys.

The same is true of the thumbplate system player wishing to transfer to the Conservatoire system. The German system has largely fallen into disuse, though there are still a handful of oboists of the older generation who make use of it. The Vienna Philharmonic is an exception to this; to this day its oboists play on the improved version of the classical model and comply with the special requirements of its fingering technique. Recently the Viennese oboe has come back into favour and there have been attempts to apply French fingering technique to it.

Remarks on Breathing Technique

All double reed instruments have a relatively small mouthpiece. This has its advantages and disadvantages. The advantages are as follows:

1 A relatively small amount of air is required to play the instrument, though this increases with the size of the reed.
2 The size of the mouthpiece and the small amount of air required means that one can play very long passages without interruption.
3 The double reed makes the construction of very low instruments possible. The amount of air required by other

The long oboe solo in the second movement of the Unfinished Symphony.

Franz Schubert (1797–1828)

contrabass wind instruments such as the tuba, the contrabass trombone, the contrabass clarinet or the contrabass saxophone is sometimes so great that longer held notes or tied notes over several bars are virtually impossible to play. Admittedly, double bassoons are not as loud as the other instruments mentioned.

Yet one should not play down the disadvantages:

1 The relatively high pressure in the oral cavity.

2 The relatively small amount of air required, which prevents the player from breathing in properly. Faulty breathing technique can lead to surplus stale air remaining for too long in the lungs without supplying them with oxygen.

3 'Hyperventilation', which can easily occur as a result of faulty breathing technique. This happens when the pupil keeps breathing in without now and again expelling the air in his lungs.

Thus it is important that, from the first lesson, great emphasis should be placed on correct breathing technique. Most tutors begin with long held notes designed to inculcate the basics of breathing technique. Pupils who have previously learned to play the recorder – an instrument which in the recent past has become increasingly important in musical education – must of course first adapt to the much higher air pressure and learn to take deep breaths.

One should get used to marking the notes with the appropriate breathing signs right from the start, making sure that the player really observes them. The narrow bore makes it possible to play for a long time without taking a new breath – one hardly ever uses up all the reserves of air in the lungs – yet the lack of oxygen which results can easily lead to tiredness and lack of concentration, and the pupil will then tend to make more mistakes because

Part of the cor anglais solo from the tone poem 'The Swan of Tuonela' *(in F).*

Jean Sibelius (1865–1957)

The composer added the following preface to the work. 'Tuonela, the kingdom of death – hell in Finnish mythology – is surrounded by a broad stream of black water and treacherous currents; on it the swan of Tuonela proceeds majestically and sings.'
This swan is symbolized by the melody of the cor anglais.

he finds it difficult to keep his mind on the music in front of him.

Of all the woodwind instruments the oboe is without doubt the one that can hold a note longest and play a long melody without interruption. In Franz Schubert's Unfinished Symphony, for instance, there is a lengthy solo passage which, depending on the speed chosen by the conductor, can last between 40 and 45 seconds. The player hardly has a chance to breathe properly because the musical line does not permit it. It is possible, however, to play this solo in one breath if one husbands the air at one's disposal carefully, and if one does not overdo the crescendo, which is not called for at this point in any case.

Whereas the oboist can play this line without taking a new breath, the average clarinettist finds it much more difficult; as a rule he has to breathe two or three times in the course of the passage. Yet a growing number of musicians have developed a special breathing technique, especially in jazz. Circular breathing, as it is called, makes it possible to take a new breath without interruption, no matter whether the music permits the player to do so or not. It may be objected that this is inconceivable – in the final analysis it is impossible both to breathe in and to breathe out at the same time; many people find it difficult to make head or tail

198

of this technique. Thus the Bremen State Philharmonic Orchestra was once rehearsing Jean Sibelius's tone poem *The Swan of
Tuonela*. In this work there is an obbligato solo for cor anglais, a
solo passage that scarcely gives the player a chance to breathe.
For this reason the conductor usually comes to an agreement
with the player on where exactly he is going to take breath; this
enables him to hold back the next beat a little in order to give the
player a chance to breathe.

In this orchestra Kammermusiker Wolfgang Hoth had perfect
command of the circular breathing technique, and, because by
nature he is a reticent man, he said nothing about the problem of
breathing in this passage. But after one of the rehearsals the
conductor came up to him and said,

'Mr Hoth, we've still got to agree on where you're going to
breathe, so that I can hold the orchestra back at these points.'
'Don't worry, I'll manage it.'
'Yes, but haven't you got to breathe somewhere?'
'No, no. No problem.'
'Wait a minute. Isn't that the place where you breathe?'
'No, I'm afraid it isn't.'
'Then what about here?'
'Not there either.'
'Well, you must have taken a new breath by this point.'
'No, not there either.'
'Yes, but surely you've got to breathe somewhere?'
'I breathe as I go along.'
'You what?'
'Yes, while I'm playing.'
'But that's impossible!'
'No, it isn't.'
'Well I never. You'll have to show me how you did it.'

The part for the two oboes in 'Passepied II' from the Ouvertüre (Suite) No. 1, BWV 1066.

Johann Sebastian Bach (1685–1750)

It should be added that if one practises a great deal – and sometimes one has to practise for years – one can become so good at this that an onlooker has to be very observant indeed to notice when the musician is in fact breathing through the nose. But once one has mastered the technique it probably helps to prolong one's life, for while the oboists on the other desks are suffering and out of breath when playing difficult parts – and here I am thinking of pieces such as the *Meistersinger* prelude, the cantatas and suites of Bach or the oratorios of Handel – the 'expert' can maintain his normal breathing rhythm by breathing 'continuously' through the nose. The conductor told us the next day that he had spent the whole night trying to imitate this technique.

Our anatomy enables us to breathe even when, for example, we are drinking something or when our oral cavity is full of water. At such moments we breathe through the nose. Normally the teacher will try to get his pupils to breathe through the mouth, but when we are trying to play this is simply not possible. But just as the oral cavity can be filled with water, it can also be filled with air while we are breathing through the nose. The reader is invited to try this out by filling his mouth with water, breathing and – perhaps with the help of a straw – attempting to shoot out a steady stream of water using cheek pressure. This is precisely what one has to practise in circular breathing, though here one is not dealing with water, but with the air remaining in the oral cavity. In the case of the oboe, as we have seen, one only needs a relatively small amount of air, and thus the air in the oral cavity suffices in order to enable one to breathe in through the nose, that is to say, via the 'back door'. The main difficulty is that we have to switch from abdominal support, which helps to stabilize the note and the tone colour, to lip pressure.

A third factor that influences the note is the position of the palate. While we are breathing through the nose the abdominal support disappears completely, and this can lead to a marked and noticeable drop in pitch, particularly if one is using a note on which to breathe that is difficult to keep in tune anyway. This technique can also be used on the bassoon, though here one has to avoid the low notes that require a lot of breath; the air supply in the oral cavity might be insufficient and lead to an interruption of the note in spite of all one's efforts.

This breathing technique has a very long history; the Greeks probably employed it; and the construction of the wind-cap instruments, and also of the bagpipes, is nothing other than an attempt to make longer passages playable without having to take a breath now and again. In the case of the bagpipes the player replenishes the bag through a blowpipe, and the chanter is supplied continuously with air by compressing the bag. Thus the reed is not dependent on the unequal pressure of the player's breath.

Whereas all folk musicians in south-east Europe are familiar with the technique of circular breathing, it is more the exception than the rule in the rest of Europe (though Arab musicians also employ it). In addition to popularizing the oboe on account of his phenomenal mastery of the instrument, Heinz Holliger has also done much to further this breathing technique. In fact for certain avant-garde works it is simply indispensable, and in the first decade of this century Richard Strauss was already writing passages for woodwind or wind in general which can to all intents and purposes only be performed with its help.

In the introduction to the *Alpensinfonie* there is the following note: 'Samuel's aerophone is to be used when the wind perform the long held notes'. What was Samuel's aerophone? In fact nothing more than a small foot-operated bellows – similar contraptions are used nowadays to blow up inflatable mattresses. At one end of the tube there was a thin mouthpiece, which supplied the oral cavity with air. When this wondrous invention was first tried out the following mishap occurred. The musician concerned, an oboist, was demonstrating the gadget to an incredulous group of experts. In his excitement he placed one of his feet on the tube conducting the air to his mouth, yet he only noticed this after he had started to play and no air came through. Though perplexed, he did not wish to compromise the success of the gadget, the efficacy of which he wished to prove, and thus he fell back on his circular breathing technique, and no one except the person telling the story apparently noticed it. Like so many other innovations this has also disappeared, and the effects intended by Richard Strauss are nowadays rarely heard.

Vibrato

Posture plays a crucial role in breathing. One keeps seeing amateur players blowing away in a crouched position, but in fact one should get used to sitting up straight, only leaning back in one's chair when one is not playing. The elbows should not rest on the body, for otherwise they will impede the movement of the breast. The position of the head should be such that one can breathe freely. One often sees players with heads bent downwards – this is also wrong, for it prevents one building up a column of air with abdominal support.

A reed that is too 'heavy' quickly leads to a cramped posture. The elbows cling to the body and prevent the player from breathing freely. Photos: Joppig.

A good indication of whether one's breathing technique is correct and, above all, that this kind of support exists, is whether a pupil can play a natural vibrato that emanates from the diaphragm. Vibrato playing produces all sorts of oddities. There are musicians who move the instrument slightly from one side to the other, and others who seem rather to be shaking it. Others again play a tremolo on the keys; and finally there are those who produce a laryngeal vibrato that not infrequently sounds like bleating. Vibrato technique can best be studied by watching singers – indeed, oboists and bassoonists can learn a lot about the shaping of musical lines by observing singers of the corresponding vocal range.

There are people who do not find it difficult to produce a vibrato from the word go, and who can also produce the effect on the instrument. Others have to practise for a long time, and certain players never seem to have been shown how to do it at all. Yet one should be able to apply vibrato when the music requires it. On notes that begin pianissimo and then get louder, one should not play vibrato from the very start; it is better to start non-vibrato and to let the vibrato develop together with the increase in dynamics.

If you wish to learn the technique of vibrato you should think of a situation where your diaphragm really hurts – this always happens when one laughs a lot and subsequently has a sort of abdominal cramp. These involuntary movements of the diaphragm can also be induced consciously, i.e. by means of the kind of exercises choirs use when warming up, which stimulates the diaphragm by the repetition of certain notes and syllables. The vibrations of the diaphragm can be transmitted to the voice fairly easily, and one only has to make a conscious effort to transfer them on to the instrument when playing a single held note. This can be done by inducing the vibrations of the diaphragm in slow succession, and thus producing rapid fluctuations in pitch.

With a bit of practice one will also be able to use vibrato on held notes within a piece, though it should be added that one must always be in a position to play without vibrato. Not infrequently one hears oboists who play vibrato all the time, which, particularly in technical passages, can sound rather odd. It is the oboist who has to give the 'A' to the rest of the orchestra; but if he uses too much vibrato on the a' the other players will find it very difficult indeed to deduce the real pitch. In addition to this, one player's vibrato can mar the effect of held wind chords, for not all woodwind instruments can play vibrato. In the case of the clarinet vibrato is very much a matter of taste – some musicians reject it categorically, particularly those who play the German clarinet. Boehm clarinet players use vibrato just as much as flautists and oboists, and it hardly needs to be said that jazz clarinettists are past masters of this technique.

The bassoon, particularly in the high register, can easily begin to sound a bit like the saxophone if too much vibrato is employed. A wise player will use it sparingly. French bassoonists tend to use vibrato more than German bassoonists.

Attack
As we have seen, more and more pupils are switching to the oboe from the recorder. The fact that children who play the latter tend

Carl Maria von Weber (1786–1826)

Beginning of the overture to the opera
Der Freischütz.

to blow softly into the instrument means that many beginners on the oboe or the bassoon do not know the right kind of attack.

One should not make light of this kind of shortcoming, for mistakes that creep in at an early stage are extremely difficult to correct later on. With regard to attack, it is important that the pupil should understand the point of the whole exercise. All double reed instruments have short starting transients, i.e. the full overtone structure of a note is present after a few milliseconds. For this reason it is extremely difficult for the oboe or the bassoon to enter from nothing, as it were, as flautists and clarinettists are able to do in such a masterly manner. And for the same reason it is common practice at the beginning of the *Freischütz* overture that the oboes, which, according to the score, should join in on c′ from the beginning, only enter in the course of the first bar after the orchestral crescendo has begun to build up. In avant-garde works one keeps coming across directions such as 'attacca from nothing' or 'enter senza attacca', but many composers are obviously unaware what this means in the case of

205

double reed instruments. A wind player who synchronizes his entry with the conductor's beat cannot simply blow into his instrument and wait for the reed to begin to vibrate; he has to keep the airstream under control with the help of his tongue by placing the tip of it at the top of the lower half of the double reed, releasing the double reed by withdrawing it the moment he wishes to play. True, the tutors recommend saying the letter 'd', yet this is not really possible, for in the case of the plosive 'd' the tip of the tongue is behind the top incisor teeth – and once one has placed the reed in one's mouth the tongue lies under the reed.

It is a much better idea to explain to the pupils what a plosive is. I usually do this by getting them to 'stammer'. They soon notice how a stammerer's tongue is an impediment to speech. If the pupil now places the tip of his finger in his mouth and repeats the whole procedure, he will feel the movement of the tip of his tongue as impulses on the fingertips. This 'tongue training' should then be repeated with a reed; the pupil will usually get the hang of correct tongue attack after a few attempts. As the lessons progress the teacher must ensure that the pupil remembers and continues to use the technique thus acquired. Incorrect attack should not be tolerated from the start. Practising tongue attack should in fact never be neglected, for double reed players always have problems with fast staccato passages. Rapidly attacked low notes are especially difficult and will only sound convincing if the player's technique is good enough.

Double-tonguing is another technique that is infrequently used on double reed instruments. Flautists and brass players (especially the higher instruments) take this in their stride, and tutors devote lengthy chapters to it. It is far less common in the case of oboists and bassoonists; in fact, there are probably only a handful of instances in the Romantic and classical repertoire that really require double-tonguing. A good oboist can also play feared passages such as Rossini's *Silken Ladder* without using double-tonguing. Furthermore, on the oboe throat attack does not respond as clearly as tongue attack, so that when practising this technique one should try to combine throat attack with soft tongue attack.

This is quite different in the case of brass instruments and flutes, where the distinction between tongue and throat attack is not as apparent. Ever since the music of the avant garde at the beginning of the 1950s began to make increased use of oboe instruments – in part due to Heinz Holliger and Lothar Faber – performers have increasingly been called upon to make use of this technique. Flutter-tonguing, where the tongue vibrates against the aperture of the double reed, is another technique that one has to be able to use in this kind of music.

It is essential that the pupil learns the techniques discussed above – circular breathing, double-tonguing and flutter-tonguing. Experience teaches one that musicians find it more difficult to learn them in later life, whereas very young pupils often pick them up in passing or acquire them very quickly. For example, a seven-year-old recorder player once played his little ditty to me with perfect flutter-tonguing, although he neither knew nor had had explained to him what this technique was. He had simply taught himself while experimenting with his instrument, and could not be restrained from applying it to everything.

Reed-Making for Oboe and Bassoon

The subject of making oboe and bassoon reeds can fill volumes and *has* filled volumes. The reader is referred to the following standard works on the subject.

Karl Steins, *Rohrbau für Oboen*, Bote & Bock (Berlin/Wiesbaden). This also deals with reed-making for related instruments.

Town piper's graduation certificate. Hermann Windeler (1914–82) was a well-known bassoonist and maker of bassoon and double bassoon reeds.

Hans Lotsch, *Das grosse Rohrbuch*, Das Musikinstrument (Frankfurt). A systematic introduction to the making of bassoon reeds.
Myrone E. Russel, *Oboe Reed Making and Problems of the Oboe Player*, Jack Spratt Music Co. (Stamford, Connecticut).
Christopher Weait, *Bassoon Reed-Making – A Basic Technique*, MacGinnis & Marx (New York).

The illustrations and instructions in these books describe reed-making in such detail that if one exercises a little ingenuity one can make one's own reeds without the help of others. However, making good reeds requires years of practice, and the amateur is often well advised not to embark on making his own reeds, and to find a supplier able to make the reeds he requires. Orchestral musicians sometimes do this, and co-principals in particular often earn a bit on the side in this way.

It would be an exaggeration to say that one must first fill a

Old reed-makers' advertisements in the Deutsche
Musiker-Zeitung *(1926, no. 23).*

washing basket with reeds before one has mastered the art of
reed-making, but no one would venture to deny that a lot of
experience is necessary. There are various ways of obtaining
reeds. The first is one's teacher, of course, who will either provide
his pupils with reeds he has made himself, or will recommend a
source from which they can be bought. Reeds can also be
obtained commercially, yet they often require further attention
before they can be played – some are too light, and others too
heavy.

One can also buy half-finished products, which are either
supplied as cane that has been gouged and shaped (or scraped),
which means that the musician has only to wrap them – or again
as gouged cane which can be cut into the required form with
one's own 'shaper'. French manufacturers in particular supply
good sets containing gouged and shaped cane, the corresponding
number of staples and even the right thread (including fishskin,
which is also known as goldbeater's skin).

Many professional musicians import their reed cane (its Latin
name is *Arundo donax*) directly from the growers in southern
France and split it vertically into three parts themselves. Oboes
require thicknesses of about 10 millimetres, bassoons of 20 to 25
millimetres. After having been immersed in water for some time
the wood is split open and, where necessary, cut to about the
length required to fit into the gouging machine. The inside is
planed to the right thickness with an inner gouging machine.
The thickness of oboe reeds varies from 0.4 millimetres (light
reeds) to 0.6 millimetres (heavy reeds). Bassoon reeds vary from 1
to 1.2 millimetres.

Whereas an inner gouging machine makes sense for someone
who does not want to rely on other suppliers and who wishes to
try out his own thicknesses, an outside 'profiler' that removes the
outside to the required contoured bevel really makes economic

sense only in the case of professional musicians who make reeds on the side or for a living. Even if one has access to a 'profiler' there is still a lot of detailed work to do before one has a finished reed. Furthermore, new reeds change after they have been played in. One is continually having to tinker with a reed, and to cut or scrape something off if it has become too heavy. For this reason every oboe and bassoon player should at least possess a good knife and an agile tongue.

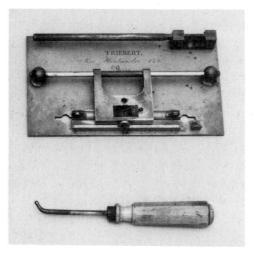

Gouging machine by Triébert, Paris, designed for filing the wood of the oboe reed to the required thickness after it has been trimmed with the cutter to the required length.
Photo: Sotheby's, London.

It also makes sense to build up a small stock of good reeds in order to avoid getting into difficulties in the middle of a concert – one's only good reed may suddenly and for no good reason give up the ghost or be inadvertently damaged. Of course other materials have been tried out in the attempt to replace the natural one, yet the former have not managed as yet to replace

210

the latter. Under certain circumstances the beginner may find it useful to play on fibreglass reeds, which do not have to be moistened. The tension remains fairly constant over a long period, which is normally not the case with other kinds of reed, especially where beginners are concerned. Problems have actually only arisen because fibreglass is evidently not elastic enough to produce the required vibrations, especially in the case of high notes, so that some of these will tend to be on the flat side. These fibreglass reeds are however quite suitable as practice reeds.

With regard to the related instruments such as the oboe d'amore, the cor anglais, the heckelphone and the double bassoon, only a handful of professional players or amateurs make their own reeds if they only occasionally play these instruments; the relatively high cost of the tools does not justify the small number of reeds required. Here the best thing to do is to get in touch with a specialist in the local orchestra, who will usually be prepared to make the reeds you need when he is making his own.

Nowadays a number of small firms that advertise in specialist journals supply reeds of varying thicknesses. Yet reed-making has not become a mass industry. True, some firms make large numbers of clarinet and saxophone reeds using the most modern technology – the insides of the reed are polished with diamonds and the reed itself accurately machined to within a hundredth of a millimetre. But this procedure has not as yet been applied to double reeds.

Having digressed to examine some of the problems of playing the oboe and the bassoon, particularly as they affect beginners, we have reached the end of this survey of the history of the two instruments. In this concise sketch of their development over the centuries the author has considered it to be of importance to give an idea of the musicianship of those who played these instru-

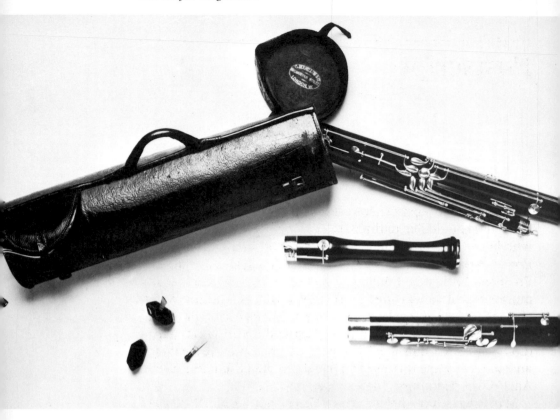

The outfit of a bassoonist a hundred years ago. Leather cases of this kind were evidently only in use in England. In Germany wooden cases tended to be used when transporting the instrument. The bassoon (serial number 481) comes from the factory of Charles Mahillon (1813–87), Brussels. In 1844 he opened a branch of his firm in London. (Gunther Joppig Collection.) Photo: Koopman.

ments. Music history has a penchant for concentrating on the big names; yet in the process it tends to neglect the players whose skill made this history possible in the first place. The great composers who now seem to us to be of superhuman stature were often on friendly terms with the performers to whose virtuoso playing they owed their early fame.

We are gradually beginning to realize, particularly in the area of music sociology, that the general social conditions and the constraints to which musicians were subject in the past, did in fact have an influence on the music itself. And in this book it was one of the author's principal aims to emphasize the skill and musicianship of past generations of players by referring to and quoting those primary sources capable of illustrating these insights.

212

Postscript

At the end of this brief survey of the history of the oboe and the bassoon I should like to thank the many people and institutions who have helped me and supplied information. I am grateful to Professor Constantin Floros, Professor Andreas Holschneider and Professor Wolfgang Dömling for their encouragement of my musicological endeavours. I also owe a debt of gratitude to my oboe and bassoon teachers – Kammermusiker Alfons Czaja and Kammermusiker Wolfgang Hoth (Bremen) and Werner Schulz (Cologne) [oboe and English horn]; Bernd Jensen (Oldenburg) and Manfred Ziese (Brunswick) [bassoon]; and Kammermusiker Adolf Kern (Hamburg) [double bassoon].

Many firms have helped me to build up my collection. I am particularly indebted to the firm of Wilhelm Heckel in Wiesbaden-Biebrich, to its former director Franz Groffy (1896–1972), whom I had the honour to know personally, as well as to the present owners, Mr and Mrs Adolf Gebhard, and Mrs Edith Reiter.

Peter Bertram of the firm of Musik-Bertram in Freiburg im Breisgau helped me to acquire some rare oboe instruments from the United States. I am also grateful for advice given by the firms of Walter Püchner and W. Schreiber (Nauheim), Buffet Crampon (Paris), Gustav Mollenhauer & Söhne (Kassel) and Richard Müller (Bremen). Sotheby's (London) kindly provided pictures from its important musical instrument-auctions.

Dr Moeck of the firm of Moeck (Celle) kindly supplied some of the pictures included in this book; and my fellow collectors Ernst W. Buser (Binnigen/Switzerland), Karl Ventzke (Düren), Pastor Günter Hart (Peine), Gerhard Hase (Stuttgart), and William Waterhouse (London) permitted me to make use of parts of their collections.

The following institutions helped with information and pictorial material:

213

Bernisches Museum, Berne

Bildarchiv preussischer Kulturbesitz, Berlin (Mrs Klein)

Beethoven-Haus, Bonn (Professor Martin Staehelin)

Germanisches Nationalmuseum, Nuremberg (Friedemann Hellwig)

Museum für Kunst und Gewerbe, Hamburg (Dr Hermann Jedding)

Musikinstrumenten-Museum, Leipzig (Dr Herbert Heyde)

Bibliothek des Hessischen Landesmuseums

Bibliothek des Musikwissenschaftlichen Instituts, Hamburg (Mrs Förtsch)

Staats- und Universitätsbibliothek Carl von Ossietzky, Hamburg (Mrs Heim)

University of Pennsylvania (University Museum)

I am particularly grateful to Beatrice Frehn and Per Koopmann (Hamburg) for their excellent photographic work.

Gunther Joppig

Encyclopedias and Dictionaries

BLUME, F., *Die Musik in Geschichte und Gegenwart*, Kassel, 1949–79

BÜCKEN, E., *Handbuch der Musikwissenschaft*, Postdam, 1927–34

FRANK, P. and ALTMANN, W., *Kurzgefasstes Tonkünstler-Lexikon*, Regensburg, 1936

LANGWILL, L.G., *An Index of Musical Wind-Instrument Makers*, Edinburgh, 1980

LAVIGNAC, A. and DE LA LAURENCIE, L., *Encyclopédie de la musique et dictionnaire du Conservatoire*, Paris, 1921–31

RIEMANN, H. and EINSTEIN, A., *Riemann Musik-Lexikon*, Berlin, 1922

RIEMANN, H. and GURLITT, W., *Riemann Musik-Lexikon*, Mainz, 1959–67, 1972, 1975

SACHS, C., *Real-Lexikon der Musikinstrumente*, Berlin, 1913; reprint, Hildesheim, 1964

SADIE, S., *The New Grove Dictionary of Music and Musicians*, London and New York, 1980

SADIE, S., *The New Grove Dictionary of Musical Instruments*, London and New York, 1984

Notes

1 Heinz Becker, *Zur Entwicklungsgeschichte der antiken und mittelalterlichen Rohrblattinstrumente*, Schriftenreihe des Musikwissenschaftlichen Instituts der Universität Hamburg iv, Hamburg, 1966
2 Curt Sachs, *The Rise of Music in the Ancient World: East and West*, New York, 1943, p. 73
3 Kurt Lange and Max Hirmer, *Ägypten. Architektur, Plastik, Malerei in drei Jahrtausenden*, Munich, 1980, p. 93
4 C. Sachs, op. cit., p. 71
5 *The Odes of Pindar including the Principal Fragments with an introduction and an English translation by Sir John Sandys*, London, 1919, p. 311 (translation slightly amended)
6 *The Iliad of Homer*, translated into English Prose by Andrew Lang, Walter Leaf and Ernest Myers, New York, 1966, (translation slightly amended), pp. 135–6
6a Ibid., p. 269
6b Hesiod, *The Homeric Hymns and Homerica with an English Translation by Hugh G. Evelyn-White*, London, 1950, pp. 239–41 (translation slightly amended)
6c Herodotus, with an English translation by A.D. Godley, London, 1950, p. 207 (translation slightly amended)
6d Thucydides, *The Peloponnesian War*. The definitive translation by Benjamin Jowett, London, 1960 (translation slightly amended)
7 Pausanias, *Guide to Greece. Vol. 1: Central Greece*, Harmondsworth, 1971, p. 333
8 Günther Wille, 'Rom', *Musik in Geschichte und Gegenwart xi*, Kassel, 1963, p. 666
9 See Edward Tarr, *Die Trompete. Ihre Geschichte von der Antike biz zur Gegenwart*, Berne, 1978, p. 32
10 On this point see Raymond Meylan, *The Flute*, Edward Tarr, *The Trumpet* and Kurt Janetzky/Bernard Brühle, *The Horn* (also published in this series in English translation, London, 1988)
11 C. Sachs, op. cit., p. 277
12 Francis W. Galpin, *Old English Instruments of Music, their History and Character*, fourth edition, revised with supplementary notes by Thurston Dart, London, 1965, p. 118
13 Walter Salmen, *Der fahrende Musiker im europäischen Mittelalter*, Kassel, 1960, p. 161f.
14 H. Becker, op. cit., p. 158f.
15 W. Salmen, op. cit., p. 213
16 *See* E. Melkus, op. cit., p. 37

17 *See* Marianne Bröcker, *Die Drehleier. Ihr Bau und Ihre Geschichte*, Vol. 1, Bonn-Bad Godesberg, 1977

18 *See* Friedrich Jacob, *Die Orgel*, Berne, 1976

19 W. Salmen, op. cit., p. 111

20 *See* Josef Ulsamer and Klaus Stahmer, *Musikalisches Tafelkonfekt*, Würzburg, 1973

21 Michael Praetorius, *Syntagma musica*, Vol. 2, *De Organographia*, Wolfenbüttel, 1619; facsimile edition, ed. Willibald Gurlitt, Kassel, 1964

22 M. Praetorius, op. cit., p. 36f.

23 F. Galpin, op. cit., p. 122f.

24 Philip Bate, *The Oboe. An Outline of its History, Development and Construction*, London, 1975

25 Albert Reimann, *Studien zur Geschichte des Fagotts. 1. Das < Phagotum > des Afranius Albonesii und zwei < fagotti > in Verona. 2. Geschichte der Namen für das Fagott*, Diss, Freiburg im Breisgau, 1956, p. 132

26 *See* Richard Schaal, 'Die Musikinstrumentensammlung von Raimund Fugger d.J.', *Archiv für Musikwissenschaft* XXI, 1964, pp. 212–16

27 M. Praetorius, op. cit., p. 38

28 Rainer Weber and John Henry van der Meer, 'Some Facts and Guesses Concerning Doppioni', *The Galpin Society Journal*, xxv, 1972, pp. 22–9

29 David Munrow, *Instruments of the Middle Ages and the Renaissance*, London, 1976, p. 50

30 Hermann Moeck, *Zur Geschichte von Krummhorn und Cornamuse*, Celle, 1971, p. 4

31 M. Praetorius, op. cit., p. 41

32 *See* Ekkehart Nickel, *Der Holzblasinstrumentenbau in der Freien Reichstadt Nürnberg*, Munich, 1971

33 Constant Pierre, *Les Facteurs d'Instruments de Musique, les Luthiers et la Facture Instrumentale*, Paris, 1893, reprint: Geneva, 1971, p. 74

34 S.A.C. Dudok van Heel and Mareike Teutscher, *Amsterdam als centrum van 'fluytenmakers' in de 17e en 18e eeuw*, Historische Blaasinstrumenten. De ontwikkeling van de blaasinstrumenten vanaf 1600. (Exhibition catalogue.) Kasteel Ehrenstein te Kerkrade 6–28 Juli 1974. Haags Gemeentemuseum, Gemeente Kerkrade, p. 54

35 Johann Christoph Weigel, *Musicalisches Theatrum*, facsimile reprint ed. Alfred Berner, Kassel, 1964

36 Heinz Becker, *'Die europäischen Oboeninstrumente' Musik in Geschichte und Gegenwart ix*

37 *See* Werner Braun, 'Entwurf für eine Typologie der "Hautboisten"' in *Der Sozialstatus des Berufsmusikers, vom 17. bis 19. Jahrhundert*, Kassel, n.d.

38 Renate Hildebrand, *Das Oboenensemble in Deutschland von den Anfängen bis ca. 1720*, Diss, Basle, 1975, p. 7. (Also in Tibia 1/78)

39 Andrew J. McCredie, *Instrumentarium and Instrumentation in the North German Baroque opera*, Diss, Hamburg, 1964

40 *See* Nickel, op. cit., p. 231f. Nickel fails to mention the bassoon in the Heckel museum in Wiesbaden-Biebrich

41 A facsimile reprint (together with Armand van der Hagen, *Méthode nouvelle et raisonné pour le Hautbois*) has now appeared. Geneva, n.d.

42 *See* Josef Marx, 'The Tone of the Baroque Oboe', *The Galpin Society Journal* (iv/1951) p. 6

43 With regard to biographical information the reader is referred to the relevant articles in *Musik in Geschichte und Gegenwart*, and in *The New Grove*

44 Percy Scholes, ed: *Dr Burney's Musical Tour in Europe. Vol. 1 An Eighteenth-century Musical Tour in France and Italy*, Oxford, 1959, pp. 57–8

45 Leo Bechler and Bernhardt Rahm, *Die Oboe und die ihr verwandten Instrumente nebst biographischen Skizzen der bedeutendsten ihrer Meister. Eine musikgeschichtliche Betrachtung*, Leipzig, 1914, p. 37

46 Karl Ditters von Dittersdorf, *The Autobiography of Karl von Dittersdorf Dictated to His Son*, translated by A.D. Coleridge, New York, 1970, pp. 47–8

47 Percy Scholes, ed: *Dr Burney's Musical Tour in Europe. Vol. 2 An Eighteenth-century Musical Tour in Central Europe and the Netherlands*, Oxford, 1959, p. 139

47a Ibid., p. 145

48 For further information on the use of the bassoon between 1600 and 1800 *see* Lyndesay G. Langwill, *The Bassoon and Contrabassoon*, London, 1971, p. 72f. and Will Jansen, *The Bassoon. Its History, Construction, Makers, Players and Music*, Buren, 1978, p. 980f.

49 Kurt Janetzky/Bernhard Brüchle, *Das Horn*, p. 52

50 Walter Kolneder, *'Fagott' Musik in Geschichte und Gegenwart iii*, p. 1726

51 Josef Sittard, *Geschichte des Musik- und Concertwesens in Hamburg, vom 14 Jahrhundert bis auf die Gegenwart*, Altona, 1890, p. 190f.

52 Both quotations come from *Allgemeine musikalische Zeitung*, Leipzig, n.d.

53 Julius Schlosser, *Die Sammlung alter Musikinstrumente. Beschreibendes Verzeichnis*, Hildesheim, 1974

54 Musikhistorisches Museum Heckel in Biebrich. Section: Bassoons, 1968, No. F7A

55 Heinrich Christoph Koch, *Musikalisches Lexikon*, Frankfurt, 1802, p. 1084f.

56 On the history of this concerto *see* Wilfried Fischer, *Johann Sebastian Bach. Serie VII. Band 7. Verschollene Solo-Konzerte in Rekonstruktionen. Kritischer Bericht*, Kassel, 1971, p. 63

57 *See* Cary Karp, 'Structural Details of two J.H. Eichentopf Oboi da caccia', *Galpin Society Journal*, xxvi/1973, pp. 55–7
58 Georg Kinsky and Hans Halm, *Das Werk Beethovens*, Munich, 1955, p. 242f.
59 *The Letters of Mozart and His Family*, Vol. 3, translated and edited by Emily Anderson, London, 1938, p. 1205
60 *See* Martin Staehelin, *Der sogenannte Musettenbass*, Jahrbuch des Bernischen Museums in Bern, xlix/1969, 1/1970, pp. 93–121
61 *See* Gunther Joppig, '75 Jahre Heckelphon. Ein Beitrag zur Geschichte der Baritonoboen', *Das Orchester*, xxviii/1980, pp. 199–204
62 Lyndesay G. Langwill, *An Index of Musical Wind-Instrument Makers*, Edinburgh, 1980, p. 151
63 Dénes Bartha and László Somfai (eds), *Haydn als Opernkapellmeister*, Budapest/Mainz, 1960, p. 47f.
64 *See* Uri Toeplitz, *Die Holzbläser in der Musik Mozarts und ihr Verhältnis zur Tonartwahl*, Baden-Baden, 1978
65 *The Letters of Mozart and His Family*, Vol. 2, translated and edited by Emily Anderson, London, 1938, p. 769
66 Hector Berlioz, *Grosse Instrumentationslehre*, ed: Felix Weingartner, Leipzig, 1921, p. xiii
67 *Richard Wagner's Prose Work*, Vol. iv, translated by William Ashton Ellis, New York, 1966, p. 298
68 *See* Walter Hermann Salagar, *Wiener Holzblasinstrumente*, Tibia, iii/1978, pp. 1–6
69 *See* Karl Ventzke, *Boehm-Oboen und die neueren französischen Oboen-Systeme*, Frankfurt, n.d. (Table iv)
70 *See* Gunther Joppig, *Die Sammlung moderner und historischer Musikinstrumente*, Glareana, xxix/2, 1980

Index